Sex, Lies, And A Charter School:
The Misappropriation of Your Tax Dollars

DIKOMBI GITE

Copyright © 2015 Dikombi Gite

ISBN: 978-0990945604

The Gite Project, LLC.
PO Box 331753
Houston, TX 77233

Dikombi@yahoo.com

Dedicated to the memory of my mother, Ruth Ann Gite (1951-1993), who has always been my guardian angel.

⚠ CAUTION

The story you are about to read will more than likely piss you off. Names have been changed to protect the innocent and guilty.

Prologue

"Hey, White, don't forget we have that meeting with Marathon this afternoon."

"The meeting is today?" I asked my colleague as he entered my office.

"Yeah, you didn't forget did you?" he asked.

"No, I'm joking with you," I replied. "My presentation is done. I need you to make some hard copies for me though."

"No problem," he responded as he exited.

I had been working for this consulting company for a little while and was quite happy with my job. After years of struggling and endless hours of being buried in the books, I finally got my degree and was working as an environmental consultant. Although the work intrigued me, I felt that something was missing.

For the better part of my life, I had this one driving goal – I wanted to be a teacher. Not just any sort of teacher, mind you. I wanted to help less fortunate kids build a future for themselves. Like many of us, I had a difficult childhood, yet I was lucky enough to receive a quality education and a financially rewarding career. However, money isn't everything as they say. And money for me was a means to an end. I wanted to have enough money to live comfortably, to offer my wife and child the home they deserved and enough savings to pursue my career of choice. I wanted to give back to my community the opportunities and support it had afforded me during my youth. I grew up in a low income community and discovered when I went off to college how disadvantaged and ill-prepared I really was. I used to tell my wife that one of the reasons our community suffers was that each generation of black people were not or could not be properly prepared by the previous generation. I always felt it was my responsibility to help and do my part.

Doing my part was going to be harder than I ever imagined it would be. There were many things that I either chose to ignore or dismiss when I began preparing to take my leap of faith. I had observed adults deny kids the bare necessities of life under the pretext of toughening them up. I had witnessed disgruntled kids navigate through life without goals or desire to be better than their elders. And I had noticed, on many occasions, adults discouraging children from taking another step toward breaking away from the mold, saying such things as, "you're not smart enough; why would you want to do that for?"

If you mix discouragement with endless rebuke, you create a child full of resentment and self-hate. When there is no encouragement, no support, no acceptance that a child's dream could become reality, the child loses hope and ceases to dream.

Therefore, my goal was to become the teacher that would encourage and give life to those seemingly impossible dreams. I would never pretend that I'm the answer or the cure to what ails our society, but if I could make a dent into the shapeless future of the children of my community, I was ready for it.

On the other hand, there are many parents who want the best for their children. These parents try their best to foster the proper growth in their kids, yet to accomplish their goals; they need the help and constant assistance of worthy educators. These educators, these teachers need to raise the children under their care from the mire of their disadvantaged station to the top of the heap. It is not an easy task, and one that would take strength of character in view of the ever-present adversity these children face on a daily basis. I believed if I could help at least one child reach his or her graduation day with honor, I was ready to do so.

Peace and quiet

I opened my eyes to complete darkness. To my left, I heard my wife, Regina, breathing softly as she lay sleeping peacefully. *She is such a gorgeous woman,* I thought. I shook my head. *How lucky can one man be?* To my right, I could hear the ticking of my watch. It read 4:29am.

Today is the day, I mused as I turned off the alarm clock before it disturbed anyone. I could feel my heart beginning to pound fiercely in anticipation of the day ahead. The journey was about to begin. I could feel the butterflies flutter their wings rapidly in my stomach. I was nervous. Part of me wanted to stay in bed and think about this whole thing once more, but there was no use, destiny was calling and I had to allay the fears of uncertainty and get moving.

I pushed the covers to one side, got up and placed my eyeglasses across the bridge of my nose before I looked out the window of our bedroom. There was no movement out there. The street light in front of our house was casting its rays over the tranquility of the early hours of the morning.

"Are you ready?" Regina whispered, when she came to stand behind me.

"Didn't know you were awake," I replied, turning to give her a peck on the forehead.

"I am just as excited as you," she said, smiling up at me.

"I guess I have to be ready. If I'm not, they will know. Lord knows I don't want that."

I walked into the bathroom and turned on the shower. The floor was cold, which woke me or threw me back into the reality of what I was about to face.

Not so bad looking for an old guy, Mr. White, I thought as I looked at my reflection in the mirror. Truth being told, I wasn't old at all, although my hair was cropped extremely short to hide my receding hairline and the stubborn grey strands that were beginning to congregate towards the front of my scalp. I smiled and shook my head. I felt on top of the world actually. The day had finally arrived when I was about to take the first steps towards achieving my goal. My goatee was finely edged, but something bothered me. *I do not like my eyeglasses,* I groaned to myself, *they make me look mean and too serious. They also make my thick eyebrows look even thicker.*

Still lost in thought, my tired, old glasses in hand, I came out of the bathroom and looked at the clothes laid out on the bed. I was very much aware of the choice I had made. I knew all eyes would be on me, so I had to make sure my appearance was on point. My white buttoned-down shirt was crisp and black sweater vest fit smoothly. My gray slacks were creased and black shoes were polished.

I shot a glance at myself in the mirror, and nodded. I looked good. I felt good. My armor was complete.

In my line of work, first impressions are very important.

"Well, look at you, Mr. White," Regina said. "Make sure they know you have a wife."

"Don't worry, love," I joked. "I'm pretty sure no one will be interested in this old man."

I quickly ate the breakfast Regina had prepared for me, and went back up the stairs to kiss my sleeping daughter before I had to leave.

"See you this evening," Regina said. "This time next year we will be calling you teacher of the year."

"We'll see what happens," I replied. "I just hope I make it to next year," I added with a smirk crossing my lips, as I passed the threshold of our home.

Looking in the rearview mirror as I left the driveway of my house, I smiled at Regina and wondered what stories I would bring home that evening.

I live in Katy, Texas, which is a suburb of Houston. The school where I was about to begin teaching was located in downtown Houston, so, with the early morning traffic, it was going to take me an hour to get there. This would give me plenty of time to get mentally prepared and churn all of these misgivings out of my head. Before I knew it an hour had passed and I had arrived at the school.

I parked my truck in front of the church. Yes, the school was actually located in a church. This was to be a temporary arrangement, but one that would cause teachers and staff some grief from time to time. Perhaps going to school in a church would give some of the wayward students cause to pause I thought. However, such was not to be the case, as I soon found out.

The school I was to begin teaching was a part of a free nationally recognized charter school system, dedicated to students living in underserved areas where public schools have traditionally failed. These charter schools are not your typical schools. They are known for their out-of-the-box teaching. During the week, the normal school day starts at 7:30am and lasts until 5:00pm. On Saturday, classes are taught between 9:00am and 1:00pm. Our school is an inner-city middle school for grades 5 through to 8.

I initially started working for the school part-time on Saturdays, teaching the kids Microsoft PowerPoint. I would bring in other professionals so the kids could be exposed to more than the negative images that they were accustomed to seeing. As a child, this was something that motivated me to be successful. A gentleman from IBM would come to our school once a week and talk about what it would take for us to make it in today's society. He was well-dressed and very articulate. I had decided at an early age that I wanted to walk in his footsteps and mentor kids.

When I interviewed for the job, I met Mrs. Robinson. We hit it off immediately and discovered we were the same age and actually attended the same high school. Ironically, we had never met. While I was teaching Saturday school, she kept telling me how they really needed more male teachers in this community, with which I agreed. I guess Mrs. Robinson had sensed this which was why she relentlessly tried recruiting me until I finally gave in to her pressuring requests.

Of course, they couldn't just give me the job; I had to go through a formal interview. I was interviewed by Mrs. Robinson, Mrs. Deeds, the principal, and Mr. Anderson, Dean of Instruction. They grilled me for two hours. I was actually impressed with their professionalism and their rigorous questioning. Later that evening I received a call from Mrs. Robinson and Mrs. Deeds offering me the position.

Now, two weeks after the interview, I was about to enter the school building not as a Saturday instructor, but as a fulltime teacher. *This is going to be interesting,* I thought then, but I was far to surmise how "interesting" this episode of my life would become.

Addition by subtraction

"Good Morning, Mr. White," I heard a voice say as I entered the building.

"Good Morning," I replied, throwing a glance around me in search of the greeter.

It was Ms. Lloyd who spoke to me. She was standing just inside the school's main office. She heard me enter the building and presumed that it was me.

She was a short woman standing barely five feet. I suspected she was in her forties, but she looked extremely young for her age.

"Are you ready for your first day?" she asked.

"I hope so," I replied. "I'm going to be in trouble if I'm not."

"Let me show you to your classroom," she offered.

Lucky for me my classroom was right across the hall from the main office. Surely, the kids would be on their best behavior since we were near the principal's office.

"Make yourself at home, because this will be your home away from home." She and I looked around the classroom. In this rather large room, the one solitary desk had been shoved into a corner and seemed to be used to stack files and papers – clearly not its intended purpose. A partition wall had been temporarily erected to serve as a separation between this classroom and the next. Although not messy, the room was in disarray. The regular school desks had been replaced by several tables, which could sit ten to twelve students easily. These were strewn about the place haphazardly with no visible organized intent, amid dozens of chairs that didn't seem to belong anywhere. The two dry-erase boards that hung on two of the walls were perhaps the only reminder that this was a classroom and not some sort of gathering spot.

Watching my gaze and then turning towards the door, Ms. Lloyd said, "I will be right across the hall if you need anything." Suddenly, she spun on her heels and added, "Oh, I almost forgot to mention that we have a quick meeting every morning before class starts. When you're ready we'll go together if you like?"

"Sure," I said, "just lead the way – I'll be right behind you." I was secretly relieved for the reprieve the meeting would afford me before I was to face the students.

The old church refectory had been temporarily transformed into a cafeteria which was large enough to host not only staff meetings but to accommodate the students for breakfast and lunch. The streaming light from the outer wall windows enhanced the atmosphere of the place. It was by no means a quiet room – every sound seemed to echo from the walls and beams overhead. I threw a rapid glance around me before noticing that all eyes were on me as soon as Ms. Lloyd and I stepped through the double doors.

All I could do was to smile at the many faces that were mostly examining me from head to toe.

"Ah, Mr. White, nice of you to join us." The woman's voice at the head of the table resonated throughout the place. "Please have a seat." She pointed to a vacant chair at the other end of the long table.

I sat down on the indicated seat, took a notebook out of my briefcase, and after she had made the round of introductions, I began jotting down my first impression of the people surrounding the table – impression to which I added comments from time to time. Later, I added and referred to these notes on numerous occasions.

First in my line of sight was Mrs. Tasha Robinson, the woman who encouraged me to join the school. Her classroom was right down the hall from mine and I would ask her for advice every chance I got. She gave me a lot of pointers and advice on how to manage my class. She was a decent-looking woman and quite aggressive in her manners. She was the kind of woman who liked to walk into a room and command attention. She was very articulate and animated. Her husband also worked at the school as the Phys-Ed teacher.

Coach Willie Robinson was just as outgoing as his wife. He really went out of his way to make me feel welcomed at the school. It was obvious that he really cared for the boys as well.

"How's it going, White?" he asked one day, as we passed each other in the hallway.

"I can't complain," I replied, "another day in paradise."

"Let me know if you need anything. We need you to stick around longer than the last teacher."

"I sure will. I am not going to let these kids get rid of me that easy."

Mrs. Amber Deeds, our principal and the woman who had invited me to sit down initially, would be next on my list. She encouraged the idea of family. She wanted the men of the school to lead a lot of the activities, especially when it concerned the boys. She also wanted the women to play more of a motherly role with the children. She preferred to be called Ms. Deeds and not Mrs. I thought that was strange, but who am I to question it.

"Mr. White, we are not only teachers, but parents, counselors, parole officers, and confidants," she told me during the meeting. "I have a close and open relationship with all of my students. We must preach honesty, integrity and believing in yourself." This was a little spiel that encapsulated her way of thinking very well.

Sitting to her right was Ms. Ebony Kidd. She was the 8th grade English teacher and the Assistant Principal. Her son and daughter attended the school. She really believed in the mission of the school. So much so, she retained her son so he could attend when it first opened. Ms. Ebony was very articulate and her mannerisms were very feminine. I really liked her and her passion for the kids was laudable. She even allowed two other boys to live with her, because their family situations were dire.

"Mr. White, I want you to read this book when you have some time," she said one morning while handing me a book entitled, "The Prayer of Jebez" by Bruce Wilkinson. "It changed my life."

"Okay, thanks for thinking of me," I replied, taking the book from her.

Then there was Ms. Lilly. She was a funny character and everyone called her by her first name such as we did with Ms. Ebony. Ms. Lilly was a tall, skinny lady with the biggest and happiest smile you would ever see. Being from Jamaica, she had the big accent to match her loud and assertive demeanor. Her two sons also attended the school. They had *success* written all over them.

"Mr. White, have you tasted the charter school Kool-Aid yet," she always asked me. "You do realize you work for a cult now."

As for Mr. Washington, he was an older gentleman who started teaching three years ago after retiring from his job as a chemist. He was *old school* at its finest. Everything about him said "Kool and the Gang." His walk was cool. The first day I met him, he was wearing a peach-colored shirt and pant-set with alligator shoes. He drove a convertible and thought he was cool. I kept waiting for him to call someone "young blood" or "jive turkey."

Ms. Lisa Trout, sitting across from Mrs. Robinson, was a young, energetic teacher who planned to lead her own school one day. This particular charter school system groomed young teachers to become school leaders and she was on her way. She was very smart and likeable.

Another young teacher was Mr. Jackson. He had an energetic spirit in a short, stout body. He had this metro sexual thing going which I really didn't know what to make of it.

Mr. Byron Steel was the other Phys-Ed coach. He was a big guy, 6'9" and 390lbs. When we first shook hands, he almost ripped my arm off. I found out later that he was practicing celibacy, which explained all the testosterone.

There were about 26 faculty and staff members in the meeting that day. I thought that I was going to be a part of something great. It didn't take long for the school to get really interesting. Let me explain how this charter middle school functions. In its first year, they only have 5th graders. They add another grade each year thereafter, eventually resulting in having a school comprised of grades 5 to 8. The school was in its third year. I found out quickly that most of the kids that were coming to the school were what I would call "last chance kids." These were kids that had bounced around from school to school and their parents were trying to find an establishment that could handle them. Unfortunately for us, we had to take them. The other rule to being a new charter school was that we had to be fully enrolled before we were given our own campus. In our particular case, the space we rented in the church would soon be fully occupied, which meant that next year we were supposed to have our own facility.

Once the meeting was over and I had heard many remarks from various teachers that would only make sense much later, I retraced my steps to my classroom.

History not to be repeated

I was teaching fifth-grade history, which was then called "Social Justice." This class was right up my alley since I have always been big on being socially conscious and aware of one's history.

As a first year teacher, I had a lot to learn. However, I thought being able to control the class would be the least of my worries. I am not the friendliest-looking person, so I thought my hard, stern stare would impose instant obedience every time it would become necessary. I could not have been more wrong.

When I entered the classroom, I was met with about thirty screaming and talking boys who mostly sat on, or straddled the chairs that surrounded the four tables. Some of them seemed to be lounging on the tabletops, totally ignoring my presence, while others stared at me as if I had just landed from some alien planet. While none stopped their chatter, I strode to the desk, shoved some of the files aside, placed my briefcase on top of it and leaned against the edge, crossing my arms over my chest. I waited until I obtained relative quiet and then began by asking the boys who were not sitting on a chair to do so. Some shrugged and only slid their bodies off the tables to go and stand by one of the windows. Others did sit down, yet none seemed very much interested in what I would have to say for the next forty minutes.

All the motherly talk and encouragement spiels I had heard during the meeting seemed to dissipate into the fog of confusion permeating my mind at that moment. I was going to have a hard time teaching anything to these kids, I thought. And I was right.

That first day turned out to be a mess. The kids refused to do anything I asked of them. I decided that I was not going to yell and scream like I had seen the other teachers do. That did not last very long. I found myself asking the kids to be quiet and pay attention nearly all the time.

The classes were separated by gender, which eliminated some of the hassles between boys and girls that the majority of schools experience. Among the children that first retained my attention was a kid named Jason, whose parents were drug addicts and whose older brother sold drugs. So, it was down to Jason to help care for his two younger sisters. Jason was a relatively good kid, but he was a "tweener." He was well behaved when he was with the good kids, but he also hung out with the rough ones.

"What's up, Mr. White?" Jason asked with a grin on his face.

"Good morning, Jason," I replied, mimicking his grin.

"So you not going to teach us on Saturdays anymore?" His smirk didn't abandon his lips. "Are you going to be here every day now?"

"I will continue to teach Saturday school," I told him. "And yes, I will be here every day now."

"Cool," he said. "You know teaching here every day is not like Saturday school. Most kids don't act up during Saturday school."

Now you tell me, I thought.

There were also two soon-to-be prison inmates named Tyson and Vonte in my class. Tyson was one of the biggest fifth-graders I had ever met. He was twelve years old and stood at 5'9" when most of the boys were barely five feet tall. He ran the show. The other boys didn't do anything unless he said they could.

Mrs. Robinson had told me that the previous year on the bus ride home, Tyson's girlfriend decided to give him oral sex while some of the other kids on the bus watched. When the bus driver realized what was going on he stopped them and reported it to dispatch. The next day both Tyson and his girlfriend, Lisa, were separately called into the office. When questioned by Ms. Deeds, Tyson said he didn't do anything. He said Lisa had oral sex with him and he just sat there.

He said, "Besides, she is my girlfriend!"

When Lisa was questioned she didn't deny it at all. She also didn't understand why it was a problem because he was her boyfriend. However, she was upset because someone had reported what she considered normal behavior between the two of them. Ms. Deeds also questioned a group of girls that had watched the whole incident. They, too, didn't see what was wrong, but wanted to know who told on them.

I couldn't believe it. Nearly all of them were ages ten and eleven and they were acting as if this was normal behavior between boys and girls.

Vonte was Tyson's partner in crime. He was small in stature but he was older as well. I didn't know exactly how old he was, but I knew he had been retained once or twice. I knew right off the bat that those two needed to go. They were constantly bullying the other kids and didn't attempt to complete any class work. I tried to talk to both boys about their actions but they did not seem to care.

One day I spoke to Vonte about his home life. I asked about his family and he began to tell me some things.

"I live with my mother and two younger sisters," he said. "My mother's boyfriend lives with us every now and then."

"So I guess that makes you the man of the house," I suggested, trying to give him a sense of worth.

"Nah," he replied. "My mother's boyfriend runs the house. You see my chipped tooth?"—he opened his mouth and pointed to his front teeth—

"This is what I get whenever I try to be the man of the house. Besides, my mother don't like me anyway. She wants me to leave, so he can stay."

"I experienced some bad things when I was your age too," I told him. "I didn't have a good relationship with my father either."

"I guess your father used to kick your ass too."

I thought sharing this information with him would open the door to better communication, but it didn't. He was a tough egg to crack and was too far gone for my help.

These two boys' antics went from bad to worse until one morning, Tyson and Vonte decided to assault another student during lunch. Roughly six boys asked different teachers to use the restroom. Little did anyone know the boy they planned to attack was already in there. Vonte beat up the boy while the others watched. Tyson held the door closed in case someone tried to come in. When it was over, they acted as if nothing happened. The victim was so afraid that he didn't tell anyone.

Fortunately, one of the bystanders felt guilty and told the principal, Ms. Deeds. We had a meeting to discuss what should be done and I immediately suggested expulsion.

"These boys are torturing the other boys on a daily basis," I said. "I am a grown man and I don't feel safe turning my back to them."

"We should not give up on them," Ms. Ebony said. "They have nowhere else to go and I don't want to see them out on the street."

"I understand where you are coming from, Ms. Ebony," I said. "But it is simple math to me. It's addition by subtraction. Why sacrifice losing the other forty boys who want and need assistance just to save two that don't."

We argued long and hard whether to keep them or not. In the end, we decided to expel Tyson and suspend Vonte for three days.

I knew it would be a matter of time before Vonte would act up again.

Tyson's mother came to the school later that day to pick him up. She was a big woman, approximately six feet tall and easily 260 pounds. When Ms. Deeds informed her of our decision, she was not happy – obviously. She already had two older boys at home who were selling drugs and going in and out of jail.

"I don't want him to be like his brothers!" she shouted, clasping her hand firmly around the straps of the bag that hung over her shoulder.

She was very upset and cursed every teacher in the school, paying no mind to the fact that the school was located in a church.

"Mr. White, you are a terrible teacher!" she went on raving. "You don't know how to handle kids. God will deal with all of you!"

About twenty minutes after she left, we all received a text message from her. It read *God will see that we have brought harm to her and her family and he will deal with us accordingly.*

Man, was I happy to see Tyson go. The classroom just felt different. It was like a dark cloud had lifted and the sun was out. The kids seemed different. I could tell there was a huge sense of relief. However, it would be short lived because three days later, Vonte was back and mad as hell.

For the first few days of his return, he did not mingle with the other students. He stayed in Ms. Ebony's classroom the entire time. She said she wanted to give him the attention he needed. After the third day, he was allowed to mix with the girls, and was back to his old ways in no time.

"Vonte, do you understand the importance of second chances?" I asked him as I saw him going down the corridor toward the cafeteria. "You have been given another opportunity to right the ship. From this point forward you have a clean slate with me."

He saw right through me and shrugged. "Yeah right, I already talked to Ms. Ebony," he said, returning to his walking down the corridor. "She told me that she was the only teacher that wanted me back. She said she needs me to show the other teachers that she is right and I can change."

I was stunned, and stopped dead in my tracks. *Why would she undermine us to make herself look good?* Even though it was the truth to a certain extent, she should not have told him that. Now, he was going to be a model citizen for her, because he thought she cared. However, Vonte was going to be even worse with everyone else, because he thought we didn't give a damn about him. In his eyes, all we wanted was to find an excuse to expel him such as we did with Tyson.

I was really inspired by Ms. Ebony's love for the children at the school. However, I thought her love for Vonte was blinding her from reality.

Appreciate apples

A few weeks had passed and I was still trying to grasp how to teach while managing a classroom full of active – not to say unruly – kids. It seemed that the fact that we were located in a church had absolutely no effect on those kids – they still misbehaved every chance they got.

Some of these children had real problems and hid or found solutions to them by inventing some escape from reality.

Case in point was a student named RJ who was extremely disruptive. It seemed he had some imaginary friends that resided under his desk. Occasionally, I saw him talking to them. Whenever I told him to be quiet he denied talking to anyone. On one rare occasion, all the students were quiet and working on an assignment, except for RJ. He was whispering something to his imaginary friends periodically.

"RJ, I need you to keep quiet. I don't want you to disturb your classmates," I said.

He didn't respond immediately. He just kept his Rain Man like demeanor.

All of a sudden he yelled, "Shut up, niggas!"

I guess his invisible friends were talking too much. The rest of the class didn't react to the outburst. They acted as if this was normal. I wanted to say something, but if this was normal, I didn't want to disrupt the exceptionally serene environment. I was shocked, but I do believe his friends stopped talking on that day.

Trying to find a means of more personal communication with my class, I thought I could establish some sort of rapport with them if I recounted one of my stories.

"Do you all want to hear my story about apples?" I asked the class.

"Do we have a choice?" Vonte replied, snickering and looking around him for his classmates' approval. I decided to ignore him. I didn't want him to wave his evil wand of disruption at this early stage.

"I think you may appreciate this story, Vonte," I said as I looked around the class. If it weren't for Vonte's willful ignorance and indifference, I estimated that most of the kids were ready to hear what I had to tell them.

"When I was a child," I began, "my father would buy food for us and food for him. He would buy two bottles of soda. My mother, sister, brother and I would share one bottle while he had the other. We would share one box of cereal while he had his own. He would also buy sweet golden apples which I really liked. Occasionally, he would allow us to have one. I loved those apples, but my father was not one to share. When I became a man and lived on my own, I always kept a bag of apples. I remember when I landed my first "real" job. I was so emotional after receiving the offer, all I could think about was going to buy a bag of apples. I had finally made it I thought. Thank you Jesus and thank you momma is all I kept repeating. Who would have thought apples would mean so much."

After finishing my story, the room was silent. Then Vonte raised his hand.

"Yes, Vonte," I said.

Vonte calmly said, "You crying over some damn apples?"

The class let out a huge roar of laughter.

You little.... is what I kept thinking while he laughed with the rest of the class. I was furious. I must have said every profane word in the dictionary as I drove home that day. Since I lived a good distance from the school, my commute was almost two hours going home. Fortunately for my family this was just enough time for me to let out my frustration. I'm sure the people watching me on the road probably thought I was crazy. It soon became a daily routine for me to punch the steering wheel and scream when I drove home from school.

Numbed by inefficiency

I was starting to feel a little more comfortable – if such should be the word to describe how I felt as a teacher. The kids were getting worse, but I was not as rattled as before. Perhaps, I had reached a level of acceptance and closed my ears and eyes to most of what the kids were dishing out every day. I don't know if I was tired of the minimal headway I had made since my arrival, or if I was just adapting to the situation. Either way, I had established a routine for myself and even though my vocal chords got a workout every day, I felt quieter inside than I did during the first few weeks of teaching. On the other hand, my brain might have been numbed by my inefficiency – I don't know.

One day I was in my classroom during my off period getting ready for class. I could hear a loud commotion coming from Mr. Campbell's room. I was used to the loud commotions, but this time was different.

As I went to my classroom door, I saw a student running from the direction of the commotion.

"What's going on down there?" I asked.

"Two girls are fighting," the student told me.

I immediately ran down the hall to help. By the time I got to the classroom, Mr. Steel was carrying one girl out of the classroom and Mr. Campbell was struggling to hold the other. It was sheer chaos. The kids were laughing and cheering. The two girls fighting were Cassie and Frenchy. From what I could see, Frenchy got the worst end of it.

"Ain't nobody gonna mess with me!" Cassie screamed while Mr. Campbell tried to hold her.

Both girls were sent to the office to deal with Ms. Deeds. She tore into them.

"I don't need to call your mommas!" Ms. Deeds yelled. "I'm momma up here! Fight now if you want to! I dare you!"

She talked a good game and bluffed those girls pretty well. Since Ms. Deeds grew up in the same neighborhood and had attended the same type of schools, she knew how to handle them. I didn't see those girls for the rest of the day. Unfortunately, the rest of the kids were so riled up, they could not get back on task after the fight.

The next few days were more of the same without the fights. Each day I attempted to teach and the kids attempted not to learn.

One day, during my off period, Mrs. Robinson came to check up on me.

"How's it going, Mr. White?" she asked with concern. "You look a little down."

"I'm very frustrated right now," I replied. "I don't know if I can teach these kids."

"Mr. White, you have to gain the kids' trust before they will respect you. Most of them have abandonment issues and are accustomed to people coming in and out of their lives."

"I understand what you are saying," I said. "I'm still not sure if I'm cut out for the classroom."

"Well, have you ever thought about working on the administrative side of the house?" she asked. "With your background, you could really help with the business side of running the school."

"Mrs. Robinson, I will help in any way I can, but I do not want to run the school. I know the responsibilities that come with being a leader and I don't want them."

"You don't have to lead anything, Mr. White." She smiled. "You know Mr. Franks?"

"Our office manager, of course I know him."

"Well, he is going to be fired," she announced. "It seems that he made some inappropriate comments to one of the students."

"What did he say?" I inquired.

"Vonte had been sent to the office for disrupting Mr. Garrett's class. He came into the office screaming and shouting, but Mr. Franks wasn't having it. He told Vonte that if he didn't sit down and shut up he would hit him in his chest so hard that he would grow breasts. Unfortunately for Mr. Franks, Mr. Banker, was walking down the hall and overheard his remarks."

"Whoa!"

"Mr. Banker instructed Ms. Deeds to fire him immediately, no excuses."

"So I guess you want me to replace him?" I asked.

"Well, if you are interested. You may be better suited in running the day to day operations of the school as opposed to teaching."

"I need to really think about it," I said.

"Take your time. However, we need his replacement by Monday. He's going to be fired this afternoon."

"Monday? You do realize today is Friday?"

"That will give you two days to get ready," she said with a smirk.

"I guess I can do it," I said. "I will do whatever Ms. Deeds needs me to do." I thought; *they don't play around here.*

As expected, Mr. Franks was fired. Mrs. Robinson called me during the weekend to talk about what I would be doing. I was going to be responsible for record-keeping and handling operational issues.

"Who's going to take my classes?" I asked.

"Ms. Lilly will be your replacement for the time being," she said. "The kids already know and respect her, so the transition should be smooth."

I was relieved, but somewhat disappointed that I would no longer teach the kids. On the other hand, I thought they really didn't like me anyway.

That Monday was strange. I had never taken but a cursory look around the main office, but that morning, I looked around me appreciatively as I entered what was to be my "home away from home", as Ms. Lloyd had called my classroom on my first day. The old vestry, such as every other room in the church, was rather large and accommodated a couple of desks and some chairs. I turned my gaze to the file cabinets lining the outer wall near the door, which seemed to be staring at me as I took a seat behind the one desk that had been assigned to this new "administrator" – a big title for a man who was a little apprehensive. As I sat there in some sort of contemplative state, my mind went back to an hour or so earlier when I had gone to my classroom to announce my departure from teaching.

To my surprise the kids were actually concerned about my leaving them in the hands of someone else. When I had heard their various comments, I rapidly went from being surprised to being stunned by their reactions. It brought me to the point of believing that they were starting to warm up to me.

Then Vonte and his mother arrived and rapidly brought me back to reality.

"Where is Ms. Deeds?" Vonte's mother yelled as she stomped into the office. "I need to speak with her about what happened with Mr. Franks."

"Okay, ma'am, I will let her know you need to see her," I calmly replied.

"Who are you?" she said, while looking me over from head to toe.

"I am Mr. White," I replied.

"Oh, I heard about you," she said with a look of disdain. "You one of the teachers that tried to kick my son out the school. Guess it didn't work."

Vonte was smiling behind her back, enjoying every moment of this.

"Have a seat," I said. "I will call for her."

"I don't want to sit," she retorted. "I want to speak to the person who said he was going to hit my son."

Ms. Deeds didn't answer her phone, but she did send me a text. She said she was at home ill and was not coming in.

"Well, ma'am, Ms. Deeds just texted me and stated that she's at home ill," I relayed.

"I need to speak to someone about what happened to my child!" she yelled. "Get Mr. Banker on the phone. This is why I hate dealing with black people, just unprofessional."

Now, she's the one wearing low rise pants while her gut hangs from under her shirt with mix match flip flops and she's calling us unprofessional.

"Let me call the assistant principal, Ms. Ebony," I said.

Ms. Ebony didn't answer her phone either. I knew she couldn't come to the office because she was teaching a class. I felt helpless. Fortunately, Mrs. Robinson just happened to walk by the office. She saw the expression on my face and came to my aid.

"I'm back, Mr. White," Mrs. Robinson said as she entered the office. "Hello, Ms. Guidry, can I help you?"

"I hope so, since Mr. White hasn't been any help," Vonte's mother said. "What is going to be done about the man that threatened my child?"

"Ms. Guidry, he has been terminated and will not pose a threat to Vonte ever again."

"He better had been fired," Ms. Guidry declared adamantly. "All I'm saying is that y'all don't want me to come up here and act a fool."

"No we do not want you to do that," Mrs. Robinson said eloquently. "However, we do need to discuss why Vonte was sent to the office in the first place."

Vonte's mother looked appalled. "It doesn't matter why he was sent to the office. The fact is he was threatened by an adult. Don't try to put this on my baby! It's already hard enough for him since all the teachers don't want him at this school anyway. Y'all keep messing with my baby and I'm going to call the state on y'all. I'm tired of this school anyway! Y'all call me when he does something wrong, but I don't hear a word when y'all do something wrong."

Mrs. Robinson and I exchanged a look of disgust while Ms. Guidry was giving her long speech.

"Let's go, Vonte, you can stay home today," Ms. Guidry yelled. "Don't call my house asking why he's not at school either, he with me. Let's go!"

Ms. Guidry and Vonte left the office and took the dark cloud of negativity with them. I had never felt so disrespected in my entire life.

"Don't worry about it," Mrs. Robinson said with a comforting smile.

I could really count on Mrs. Robinson.

"Next time that happens call Ms. Ebony," she suggested to me. "She is supposed to back up Ms. Deeds when she's not here."

"I did, but Ms. Ebony didn't answer," I replied.

"Well…, okay then," Mrs. Robinson said, a quizzical look on her face. "I guess I will see you later."

With these words, she left me alone in the office and I felt just as lost as I was when I first arrived to the school.

Given Ms. Deeds' absence and since no one had had the time to tell me what Mr. Franks had been doing; I would have to figure out how to run the show by myself. I knew the first thing I needed to do was record the attendance. It was 8:15 am and I needed to email the attendance count to Mr. Banker by 9:00 am. This meant I had to quickly collect all the attendance slips from the teachers and call all the absent students' parents. I didn't receive all the slips until 8:45 am and I needed to call about twenty parents. There was no way I was going to make that 9:00 am deadline. It took me until 9:30 to get the email out.

Mr. Banker was not happy. He sent me a scathing email about being punctual and meeting deadlines.

Fortunately, Ms. Deeds responded to the email – from her home – telling him that I had just started the position and she would show me how to do a better job.

I felt a little relieved that she had come to my assistance. I had heard about Mr. Banker and how he ruled with an iron fist. He was a former teacher who came up with the concept of this particular charter school system. He believed he could come up with a better way to get kids prepared for college. He started with one school in a rented building and turned that into over 80 schools nationwide. He was a media darling admired by many. However, I found out quickly that he was feared by most of his employees, specifically the ones I worked with.

Whenever word got out that he was coming to the campus, it was like Darth Vader had arrived. Everyone would get into a panic.

Missing in action

After working in the office for a little while I started to get the hang of things. Parents were constantly coming into the office complaining about something.

Ms. Deeds' absence was now a routine occurrence, unfortunately. There were rumors that she and her husband were having issues. I could understand how that could happen. Being a school principal was not a simple task by any means. It demanded one to be dedicated to the children's education and their well-being. She felt responsible for them as if she was a mother to them all. Unfortunately, her dedication may have negatively affected her family life.

"Hey, Mr. White!" Mrs. Robinson said as she entered the office.

"Good morning, Mrs. Robinson," I replied with a smile.

"I have some news you may like," she said gushingly. "Ms. Deeds decided we need two people to work in the office instead of one."

"That's cool with me," I said, "because this is too much for one person."

"What if I said I was going to leave the classroom and join you in the office?" she queried.

"That would be even better. I think we could really whip this school into shape. But who's going to take your classes?"

"We have another teacher coming that I think will fit in nicely," she said. "He reminds me of you. He will be here this afternoon to complete his paperwork, so you will get a chance to meet him."

Man, they make decisions quick around here is what I was thinking.

"Okay, I will definitely look out for him," I replied, returning to the task at hand.

To enumerate all of the things that I did every day would fill an entire notebook and then some. Meeting deadlines soon began to be a burden rather than a challenge. The pressure was on every minute of the day, while phone calls and parents' complaints filled the rest of the time. So, having Mrs. Robinson join me in the office had been more than welcome news. As for "whipping the school into shape", it would take more than Mrs. Robinson and I to scratch even the surface of the problems weighing this school down.

As expected, later that day, a well-dressed gentleman named Mr. Gordon II came in. He was the new teacher. He dressed rather expensively right down to the cufflinks.

"Good afternoon, sir. My name is Mr. Gordon II," he said as he entered the office. "I have an appointment with Mrs. Robinson."

"Yes, nice to meet you, Mr. Gordon," I said, while extending my hand. "I am Mr. White. Mrs. Robinson is expecting you. Feel free to take a seat while I let her know you are here."

"Thank you," he replied as he moved toward the chair across from my desk. "How long have you worked here, Mr. White?" he asked.

"Not very long; I just started working here fulltime a couple of months back."

"What school were you working at before?"

"Actually, this is my first time working for a school. I was working as a consultant in the oil & gas industry before I took the job here."

"I'm confused," he said, apparently puzzled. "You left the oil & gas industry to work for a charter school? No offense, but did you get fired or laid off?"

"That's funny," I replied jokingly. "No offense taken. But no, I resigned because I thought this would be a good challenge for me."

"Well, if it's a challenge you want then you will definitely get it working in this field," he said with a smile.

"Trust me, Mr. Gordon, I have encountered more challenges than I could've ever expected," I said. "What school are you coming from?"

"I've been teaching at an alternative high school."

"Oh, it's good that you've had that experience because you are going to need it over here. These kids are off the chain."

We were laughing when Mrs. Robinson came in with a big smile on her face.

"Well, aren't you a sight for sore eyes," she said to Mr. Gordon. "I hope you don't plan to come to school looking this delicious every day. The women around here just might attack you," she joked. "How's your family doing?"

Mr. Gordon was blushing from ear to ear. "The family is fine," he replied.

As Mr. Gordon stood up, Mrs. Robinson grabbed him by the arm, leaving the office with a smile on both their faces. However, I could hear her talking down the hall.

"Ms. Trout, meet Mr. Gordon II," Mrs. Robinson said, a devilish tone to her voice. "Isn't he handsome?"

"Yes, indeed, yes indeed," replied Ms. Trout, stepping into the office with a huge grin on her face while still trying to look at Mr. Gordon.

"How are you, Mr. White?" she asked.

"I am excellent, and yourself? I see you met Mr. Gordon II."

"Yes, indeed, I did," she said dreamily. "He's still not as good looking as you, Mr. White."

"Now that you have twisted my arm, Ms. Trout, what can I do for you?"

"I just want to give you this bus report I received this morning."

"Some kids have been fighting on the bus. It seems Alicia Scott is the main culprit. Someone needs to call her mother and inform her that she is not allowed to ride the bus for a week."

"So, who usually makes the call?"

"Well, Ms. Deeds usually does. However, she hasn't been here for the past two days. Ms. Ebony would be next in line, but she said she didn't have time. Mrs. Robinson is busy with her class, so I guess that leaves you."

"Okay, then I'll make the call," I said reluctantly.

"Thank you, Mr. White." Ms. Trout sounded satisfied when she turned towards the door.

"How are you, Mr. Goodman?" I heard Ms. Trout ask as she left the office.

"I am better now that I have seen you, Ms. Trout," Mr. Goodman replied amicably.

"I know you are," Ms. Trout sassily said, "I know you are."

Mr. Goodman backed into the office while watching Ms. Trout walk away.

"A woman like that would give me a heart attack," he said. "How are you, Mr. White?"

"I can't complain," I responded, even though I had an infinite list of complaints – not all mine – littering my desk.

"I need to speak with Ms. Deeds," he said.

"Sorry, Mr. Goodman, she is out ill." Unfortunately this had become my routine answer.

"Again!" he sounded upset. "I tell you what. We can't have another year like last year. I won't stand for it. I have been working my tail off for this school and I need some support. The PTA can't do this alone."

Mr. Goodman was the president of our Parent Teacher Association and his wife was the secretary.

"Did Ms. Deeds tell you about the fundraiser?" he asked.

"No, I don't know anything about it." I reclined to the back of my chair, wondering what else I ought to know and had not been told.

"Well, who can I talk to if she is not here?"

"I would try Ms. Ebony," I suggested. "She is the acting principal when Ms. Deeds is not here."

"What?" he uttered as if in shock. "When has she ever acted like the principal? I've tried to call her several times but she won't return my calls."

"Well, you can talk to Mrs. Robinson."

"Mrs. Robinson…, hum, I don't like the way she talks to me. She just makes me uncomfortable. She's just too fake. I know she doesn't like me, but she acts like she does." He advanced his body in the chair and put his forearms on the desk. "Listen, Mr. White, I need some cooperation with the fundraiser this year. Last year didn't end so well. I am not pointing fingers but three thousand dollars walked away without any trace."

Whoa, I thought. *How could that have happened?*

"Well, Mr. Goodman, let's make this year better. Why don't you and I work together and I will make sure the money doesn't walk away."

Mr. Goodman paused and stared at me. "We will see, Mr. White," He sounded incredulous. Obviously he had doubts. "Okay, from now on I will only deal with you," he concluded in a huff.

"Sounds like a plan," I said.

A few weeks had passed and Mr. Gordon had settled nicely into his new classroom. The kids seemed to like him, especially the little girls. Mrs. Robinson was now working full time in the office. We worked very well together. Whenever something came up, she or I would handle it with no hesitation. Ms. Deeds' mother had a few health scares, so she was still missing a lot of school. Whenever a parent would request to speak with her, either Mrs. Robinson or myself would handle the conversation.

"Good morning, Mrs. Robinson," I said as I entered the office that day. "You are here early this morning."

"Yeah, well sometimes you have to take up the slack," she said with a little antipathy in her voice.

"You okay?" I asked.

"I'm fine, just a little irritated," she said. "FYI, Ms. Ebony is not coming in today. She fell and hurt her leg or back or whatever. If she stopped drinking so much, maybe she would not have hurt herself."

"Ms. Ebony is an alcoholic?" I blurted in amazement.

"You have never noticed how she looks when she comes to school? Her hair is never combed. Her clothes look a mess and her eyes are always glassy."

"I did notice some of that, but I thought she just had the afro-centric thing going. You know; all-natural."

"Yeah, an all-natural, hot mess," Mrs. Robinson returned, visibly annoyed. "I cannot understand why Ms. Deeds puts up with her and her sister. They are both raggedy."

I had no idea Mrs. Robinson felt this way towards Ms. Ebony and Ms. Lloyd. "Are you and Ms. Deeds really close?"

"Yes," she answered. "We have been friends for over ten years. Our families celebrate the holidays together."

"So why didn't she make you her vice principal?" I asked.

"I don't know. You will have to ask her."

Mrs. Robinson was not the vice principal, but her presence was much like that of the principal. She ran the school. She hired teachers and managed them. She pretty much did everything Ms. Deeds was supposed to do.

"Mr. White, I have to meet with the bus officials regarding a fight on the bus," she said. "I will be back in a few hours if anyone comes looking for me."

"Okay, take your time," I replied. "I'll hold down the fort."

Come-to-Jesus

As usual, every morning we had a quick teacher meeting in the cafeteria while the children ate breakfast. Ms. Deeds used this time to address some of the things that happened the day before and also things we should be aware of throughout the day. One morning before Ms. Deeds arrived, I was going through all the profile pictures I had of the teachers. I needed a picture of the staff to post on our website. I noticed that I still had not received pictures from some of the teachers.

"Excuse me, everyone," I said. "Before you all start the meeting, I need pictures from Ms. Trout, Mr. Washington and Mr. Anderson." Mr. Washington gave me this evil look.

Before I could get a definite answer as to when I could get the missing photos from them, the cafeteria doors opened and in marched Ms. Deeds. Her decisive stride arrested everyone's conversation as we turned our gazes to her.

"Okay staff, we have a situation," she said, taking her seat at the head of the table. "It seems that a website was created and one of our female students had nude pictures of herself posted. We have to get to the bottom of this. Her mother believes that Ms. Ebony's son, Charles, did it as an act of revenge."

Charles and the girl, Jillian, had been an item since they both entered the school two years ago. However, Charles decided he wanted to date someone else, so Jillian started dating one of his friends. Charles supposedly didn't take it well, which is why he was now the prime suspect.

40

"After the attendance is taken, we need to gather all the children into the cafeteria and have a 'come-to-Jesus' session," Ms. Deeds went on emphatically.

Our school principal was good at putting the kids on "blast" as she liked to call it. She knew how to get into those kids' heads; to where they would tell her everything she wanted to know. It was masterful how she would manipulate them.

So after I emailed the attendance to Mr. Banker, at 8:59 am to be exact, I went up to the cafeteria where everyone had gathered to hear Ms. Deeds' speech.

"I have a major problem, family," she yelled. "Someone has hurt a member of this family and I don't like it."

The majority of the kids looked shocked because they had no idea what she was talking about. However, there was a group of "cool" kids that did not respond at all.

"Haven't I told you that you can come to me whenever there is a problem and I would try to fix it," she went on. "I am hurt. I really am. When you hurt one of my kids, you hurt me. If you are willing to hurt me that means you don't care about me. Are we not family? What happened to love and integrity?"

There was complete silence in the room, except for Jillian's mother. She was nodding as if she was about to grab one of those kids.

As a parent I could understand the anger and humiliation, but that was where my empathy towards her ended. She was a problem parent. She complained about everything. I liked Jillian, but let's be real. She wasn't the model child. She acted much older than she needed to be and I wouldn't have been surprised if she was sexually active. She was constantly getting into arguments with teachers as well. Now, her mother felt justified in acting a fool at school.

"Now, who in this room knows what I am talking about?" Ms. Deeds shouted. "Stand if you know!" she demanded.

One by one about 20 kids stood up, all seventh graders except for one 5th grader. Ms. Deeds looked at the 5th grader named Neo.

"Tell me what happened," she said to Neo with a look of surprise.

Neo looked around bashfully and with tears starting to stream down his face. "I took an extra snack yesterday when I wasn't supposed to. And when the teacher asked who did it, I blamed it on Mr. White." He turned to me. "I'm sorry, Mr. White. I didn't mean to lie on you, I was just hungry."

I was shocked, but I was also trying to refrain from laughing. He was crying uncontrollably.

Ms. Deeds looked at him and said, "I love you, Neo. But you have to show some integrity and honesty. Mr. White was really hurt when you lied on him. I need you to write a two-page essay on why it is important to have someone trust you."

"Yes, ma'am," Neo replied between sobs. "I'm sorry, Mr. White."

"Now, I see a whole bunch of 7th graders standing up. Obviously something happened," Ms. Deeds resumed, adopting a louder and demanding tone in her voice once again.

No one wanted to say anything, they just stood silent. Noticeably, Charles was not one of the kids standing.

"I know these aren't the only ones that know what I am talking about," she added, her eyes roving around the room.

Then another 30 kids stood up, all one by one. Still, Charles did not stand. His mother was practically in tears and I felt bad for her. Charles was a decent kid, but he was always angry. Some of his reasons I could understand. His father was not with his mother and he lived in a small, crowded house. However, his mother spoiled him to compensate for what he didn't have. Ms. Deeds also spoiled him and treated him as if he were hers. She had a real fondness for boys. She didn't really like girls too much. You could see it in the way she treated her son and daughter. She adored her son, but felt burdened by her daughter.

"I want all the kids standing to go to my office right now. We need to have a talk," she said.

And just like that it was over. The kids who hadn't stood up returned to their class to speculate about what happened while the others went with Ms. Deeds.

"Hey, Mr. White, I have the scoop on what happened with Jillian," Mrs. Robinson said as she rushed into the office.

"So what happened?" I asked.

"Well, Jillian actually sent those pictures to Charles a long time ago," she explained. "It's seems that after they broke up, Jillian started dating his friend. Charles became upset and emailed them to everyone."

"To everyone!"

"To everyone," she repeated. "No one knows who actually posted the pictures on the internet."

"We will never know who did," I remarked somberly.

"She definitely knew what she was doing," Mrs. Robinson said. "She looks like a grown woman."

"You saw the pictures?"

"Yes, I have them on my computer. Do you want to see them?" she asked.

"Oh no, that's okay," I replied. "I don't want those images in my head."

Later I wondered if Mrs. Robinson was trying to test me. It didn't matter. I am not a pedophile.

"Well, Ms. Deeds decided no one will be disciplined since she doesn't know who actually posted the pictures," she concluded, seemingly displeased with the outcome of this event.

"So all that drama for nothing?"

"I wouldn't exactly say that," Mrs. Robinson said.

Some days had passed and I was becoming more "comfortable" – no misgivings here – with my new position. I don't know if the kids were starting to calm down or if I was just starting to get used to the chaos. There was an uneasy calm.

That morning, Mr. Washington came into the office on his break. "Hey, White, I'm going to leave for a bit," he said. "I will return shortly."

"Where are you sneaking off to, Mr. Washington?" I asked jokingly. He was not amused.

"I have some business to tend to," he snarled.

By now I had grown accustomed to his curtness with me. I actually attributed his attitude to his experience in Vietnam. He left the office, but returned five minutes later.

"White, I need to talk to you in the hallway," he said.

"Okay," I replied. "Let me put these files away and I will be right there."

It only took me but a few seconds to put the files away, but when I stepped out Mr. Washington was gone. *That's strange,* I thought, *but this is Mr. Washington.*

At the end of the day I went to his classroom to see what he wanted. When I got there he was on the phone.

"I'm busy right now," he said. "I will catch up with you later."

A few days later I had forgotten all about him. However, I guess he hadn't forgotten about me and decided to confront me one morning during breakfast while I was helping with the kids.

"White, I want to talk to you," he said in his 1970's pimp tone.

"What's up?" I pretended not to notice he was upset.

"I don't like the way you talk to me. You ain't my boss and I don't like you checking up on me."

I looked at him and then I looked at the two students waiting for me to check them off the breakfast list. "Mr. Washington, let's discuss this another time," I snapped.

"You don't tell me what to do, baby," he shouted. "I pegged you from day one. I know what you're all about. First, you stole my project and now you're trying to be my boss."

Project, what project? I thought.

I looked at him again and then at the students that were waiting for my response to him.

"Mr. Washington, we can't have this conversation right now," I said calmly. "Let's talk later."

By this time, the students sitting closest to me started to pay attention to what was going on.

"There you go again." He was rocking from side to side. "You half my age, baby. I ain't scared of you. You ain't gonna do nothing to me."

Now I am starting to boil. All I could think was smashing that shell-shocked Supafly right where he stood. I looked at him and then at the students.

I leaned over to him and, in a whisper, I said, "Be careful what you ask for."

"What!" he yelled. "Who are you supposed to be? You think you bad or sumthin?"

By this time, Coach Steel could hear the commotion and intervened. "Is everything alright?" he asked.

"All is well, Coach, we are just having an animated discussion," I said while eyeing Mr. Washington. "Mr. Washington was telling me a story before he needed to get back to his class."

Old Supafly wanted to curse me out so bad, but he decided just to leave instead.

Wait until school is out, I thought. *I'm going to kick his old ass.* That's right. This was about to be an old fashioned after school butt-kicking. Out of all the years I had worked in a cut throat corporate environment, I had never felt the need to physically hurt somebody as much as I wanted to hurt him.

Ms. Deeds came into the office later that day, asking about some requests she had made earlier.

"Mr. White, you look a little frustrated," she said. "Put a smile on your face."

"Yeah, well, some people around here don't like to see me smiling," I replied, not even lifting my gaze to her.

"I heard," she remarked casually.

I felt like she could sense my frustration, so I told her what happened. "I just want you to hear it from the horse's mouth before word starts to really travel. Mr. Washington and I had a disagreement this morning."

"I heard about it," she repeated. "One of the students told me about it. Don't worry about it. I'm about to let him go anyway."

I was surprised to hear that. "Why?" I asked.

"Well, it seems he has been cursing at the kids and challenging them to fights."

"What?" I said, cracking a smile. Honestly, I really didn't want him to leave because the kids needed to see more men in the school, but this guy was a little crazy.

"I will tell you more about it later," she said, retracing her steps out of the office where she met Mrs. Robinson.

"Hey, honey," Mrs. Robinson said to Ms. Deeds. "You feeling better? Why don't we leave the husbands home tonight and go out?"

"What husband?" Ms. Deeds asked abruptly. "Come back to my office when you get a chance, we need to talk."

I acted as if I hadn't heard any of that.

"Hey Mr. White! Everything going okay?" Mrs. Robinson asked, coming into the office.

"Oh yeah, all is well," I said.

"That's not what I heard." She grinned. "I heard it was about to be on and crackin."

We both let out a good chuckle.

"I guess the news really does travel fast," I said.

That evening I had another good story to tell my wife.

Be careful what you ask for

Our science teacher, Ms. Gibbons, had been in the classroom for over 40 years. She had been Ms. Deeds' mentor when she first started teaching. She was probably the most experienced and most knowledgeable teacher we had, with an expertise that could not easily be matched. With her head of white streaked hair, her arms striated with the onset of arthritis and a diminutive figure, Ms. Gibbons could be described as the fragile elderly folk that still work in the twilight of their lives. Unfortunately, the kids behaved horribly in her class, especially the girls. They wouldn't do anything she asked of them. I would have to go help settle them down from time to time, which was ironic, because they used to do the same thing to me.

It amazes me how people respect titles and not people. When I first came to the school as a "big time consultant", I was respected by both the students and their parents. When I officially became a "teacher", I was looked down upon by the same people. Now that I am in the office, I have been bumped up a notch above a teacher.

I could tell that Ms. Gibbons was starting to really dislike the kids. The way she addressed them made me feel uncomfortable. I mean, I can understand her frustration, but this was way past irritation. She was also very forgetful. Every morning someone had to remind her to retrieve her first period class from the cafeteria after breakfast.

One morning I went to her classroom to remind her that she needed to retrieve her students. She was just sitting at her desk, staring into space.

"Ms. Gibbons, don't forget about your class," I said.

She looked at me and a tear streamed down her face.

"I just can't continue doing this," she said as she began to weep.

I rushed to her side to console her a little. "It's going to get better. The kids are just acting up because it's the beginning of the year. Just wait, next year when we get our own building, things will be different. We will be able to pick and choose who we let in and they will look at us as a real school."

"You really believe that, don't you?" A veil of sadness suddenly marred the lines of her gentle face.

"Of course I do."

I gave her a big hug hoping she would get it together before the kids came. Then something strange happened. She hugged me back, but it was a different kind of hug. It was a hug like my wife gave to me. She held me, put her head on my chest and let out a sigh.

Ms. Gibbons was your typical grandmother type. I didn't know what to do. I backed up and acted as if it didn't happen. This wasn't the first time she made me feel uncomfortable, but this was definitely the closest she had ever gotten to me. She had made little comments before of how she thought I was handsome and muscular. But this was like grandma hitting on you. I hurried back to the office as quickly as I could.

"Hey, Mr. White," Ms. Trout said flirtatiously as I rushed past her in the hallway.

"Hey," I said trying not to look ashamed.

I couldn't get to the office fast enough. Mrs. Robinson was sitting at the front desk.

"You sure are moving fast, Mr. White," she remarked, lifting her gaze from her paperwork.

49

"Yeah, I just left Ms. Gibbons' room," I replied. "She's an emotional wreck."

"Oh yeah, I know." The nonchalance in her voice didn't escape my notice – *was it indifference, perhaps?*

"I think she tried to make a pass at me."

"What do you mean tried?" she said with a smirk. "She wants some of that fine, young Mr. White. She talks about how fine you are all the time."

"What, that's nasty!"

"Mr. White, she is a sixty-five year old woman who has not been with a man in I don't know how long."

"How long has she been saying this stuff?"

"Since you started working here," she laughed. "She's not the only one who has been checking you out!"

"What!" I was positively stunned.

"You have a lot of admirers around here. Just make sure you remember you have a wife and daughter at home."

I am no fool, I thought. *I have a good thing at home and I am not going to mess that up.* "I guess it's good that you and Coach Robinson work together. You don't have to worry about that kind of stuff."

"Yes, I guess. It has its positives and negatives. It's hard to work with him when I am mad about something that happened at home, but we do understand each other's frustrations with the job." She paused. "By the way, have you seen him – I mean my husband – have you seen him this morning?" she asked.

"Not yet, he usually comes in the office to talk around eleven. Did you try calling him?"

"I did, but he's not answering. Anyway, I am going to Ms. Deeds' office. And if you see Coach, tell him I want to see him, if you don't mind."

Just like clockwork, Coach Robinson came into the office around eleven.

"What's up, White!" he said as he entered.

"All is well," I replied.

Coach Robinson was a very likeable guy. He believed in what Ms. Deeds was trying to accomplish and wanted to help, so he became the Phys-Ed teacher. The kids loved him, especially the girls. They looked at him as a father figure and they also thought he was good looking.

"I just wanted to give you a heads up," Coach Robinson said. "I am expecting a large delivery of drinks and snacks today. I will be selling items during lunch and after school to raise money for the athletic program."

"That's a good idea. I will let you know when it comes."

He hesitated before he said, "I am looking for someone to coach the basketball team this year. Since you used to play basketball, I was wondering if you wanted to do it."

"Count me out," I replied firmly. "I don't have time. Between work, trying to start a business and family, I really don't have the time."

"That's cool, but if you know someone let me know." Visibly disappointed, he left the office with a shrug of his shoulders.

"Oh, Coach, Mrs. Robinson is looking for you," I said before he disappeared.

"Okay, I will deal with her later," he replied.

Basketball was a sore topic for me. I played in high school and never felt I got a fair shake. I never thought I was NBA material but I knew I could play in college. Unfortunately, my high school coach didn't think so. I was a six-foot guard playing the power forward position which didn't work out very well. I transferred my senior year to play for another school, but my old coach squashed those plans. He reported me to the school district for recruiting violations, so I couldn't play. I thought my world had ended, because I believed that was the only way I was going to go to a good college. Fortunately, my grades were pretty good, so I received an academic scholarship. When I got to college any thoughts of trying out for the team were dashed, because I blew my knee out playing pickup games. So, for years, I stayed away from the game. I really didn't watch it much after that and coaching was not in my plans.

One of the things that our school was not doing well in the past was keeping up with the accounting. Ms. Deeds explained to me that the school was over budget. "I will be the first to admit that I am not good at accounting," she said. "Somehow I went over budget by 150k after two years of the school being open."

"How did that happen?" I asked, taken aback. *$150,000; that's a heck of a lot of money to over-spend,* I thought.

"I honestly don't know," she replied. "I need you to help me with this." She began playing with the pen in her hands, as if embarrassed. "First, we need to collect lunch money from last year and make sure we stay on top of this year's balances."

"What happened to last year's lunch collection?" I asked.

"I believe a lot of parents didn't pay their balances from last year. We basically used a pen and paper to tally lunches, but unfortunately we came up short."

"Okay," I said, shaking my head. "Let me review the records from last year and I will send out statements." *$150,000 for lunch money – that's a heck of a lot,* I repeated to myself, still a bit surprised.

"All of the records you need are in my file cabinet in the back of my office," she said. "You can retrieve them whenever you have time."

Later that day when I went to Ms. Deeds' office to go through the files, Mr. Jackson was leaving as I was coming in.

"How are you, Mr. White?" he asked.

"Never better, Mr. Jackson. Another day in paradise," I replied, with a broad grin on my lips.

"You sure you don't want anymore?" Mr. Jackson asked Ms. Deeds.

"No, I am stuffed. You can have the rest," she said, handing him her leftovers.

"Man, Pappadeaux's for lunch," I said. "That seafood sure smells good."

"It tastes good too," Mr. Jackson joked as he began to eat the rest of Ms. Deeds' fish. "Anyway, I need to get back to class before these kids kill each other."

Mr. Jackson was a young guy just out of college. From what I could see he was doing a great job teaching. So much so, Ms. Deeds was really pushing him into leadership. She made him the grade level chair for the seventh grade even though there were two other well-experienced teachers she could have chosen. As I said before, he had this metro-sexual thing going. He wore his clothes a little too tight for me and liked to walk around barefoot. *Whatever floats your boat I guess?* Looking down at my attire, I had to admit that my button-down shirt and pressed slacks were definitely too conservative if compared to Jackson's artsy look.

"Did you need me, Mr. White?" Ms. Deeds asked.

"No, I was just coming to look at those meal balances we talked about," I said.

She took a moment before she raised her gaze to me. Obviously, she had something on her mind. "Mr. White, I feel like I can trust you. And I need to tell you something," she began.

I could tell this was serious, she looked shaken.

"I just want you to hear it from me before the rumors start." She paused, choking on the words. "My husband and I are going to get a divorce. He has committed adultery one too many times. We are in the process of getting separated now. I may be out for a little while because I will be moving. He can keep the house."

I could tell she was really feeling bad. She looked drained.

"I am sorry to hear that," I said evenly.

"Also, I believe Mr. Banker is looking to replace me," she said.

What? I thought. *No wonder she looks worn.*

"He has not been happy with my performance as well as the performance of the school. He believes I am not hiring the right people and I am not leading the school in the right direction. I knew this was coming though, so I am not worried."

"What are you going to do?" I asked.

"I am going to keep doing my job as long as I have it," she replied flatly.

"Well, I am on your team. Whatever you need me to do I will do," I offered.

Although she claimed to be in control, and not flustered by the whole thing, she couldn't stop from shedding a few tears before regaining some sort of composure. Ms. Deeds *was* a mess – and she was *in one* – It wasn't going to get better any time soon. This was the first time I felt a personal connection with Ms. Deeds.

"You are a strong woman and I really think you have been doing a great job. Whatever you need me to do I will," I added, as I gave her a hug.

"Thanks, Mr. White," she said, wiping away some of her tears with a tissue.

I left her office with the box of the meal records. The records were a mess. I had to go through several binders of tally sheets that showed the daily tallies of meals eaten by over 300 students. Then I had to compare that to payment receipts that had been issued. Unfortunately, I didn't have many receipts to go through. There wasn't any accounting of what had been paid last year, so I couldn't possibly know what was owed. In the end I decided to send statements for this year. Instead of recording tallies by hand, I created an electronic database so I could pull up any information I needed instantly.

Yet, I was at a loss to know how I was going to recover monies owed to the school from parents who generally have grievances at the forefront of their minds – not payment of lunch money. So, once I had entered all the data in the spreadsheet, I asked for Mrs. Robinson's assistance. She was smart and very creative.

"Do you have any ideas on how we can collect the past due lunch money?" I asked her.

"I sure do. Let's schedule a field trip and stipulate that all balances have to be paid in order to go. Parents are going to line up out the door so their children can go."

"I like the way you think, Mrs. Robinson," I chuckled.

The next week we did exactly that. After I calculated all the outstanding balances, I sent letters to the parents detailing the field trip to the skating rink and that their past due balances had to be paid for their children to attend. A few parents called irate, but decided to pay.

However, the payments were not coming in as I would have expected. "We aren't getting much of a response," I said to Mrs. Robinson.

"Just wait until the day we leave," she suggested.

She must have had a crystal ball, because parents filled the office the morning of the trip.

"This is a bunch of bullshit!" one father said as he waited in line.

"I can't believe they are not going to allow my daughter to go because of some little lunch bill," one mother said.

"Mrs. Robinson, I think this is very unprofessional and I would like to speak with Ms. Deeds," another mother demanded.

I had been warned about this woman. Her name was Ms. Russell. She was a large woman – at least 350lbs. – with a huge head of weave, and wore blue contact lenses, which looked abnormal – not matching her features as God had intended. She was clearly a diva and thought she was better than us low level teachers.

"I demand to speak to someone about this. I do not believe I should have to pay this bill." She owed two hundred dollars and thought that was too much. "Isn't my daughter supposed to be on free lunch?"

She is a total fraud, I thought. *Here she is questioning our professionalism and she was trying to get free lunch*. She had a fulltime job and lived with her mother. She clearly was spending a lot of money on her clothes, hair and nails.

"Well, Ms. Deeds is not in today and neither is Ms. Ebony," I said. "I can address any of your concerns and we can go over my records. Then you can have a better understanding of how I came up with that balance."

"I don't have time for all that," she retorted impatiently.

"Well, if you feel you should be getting free lunch, you can complete this application and provide proof of income." I handed her the form. "Then your daughter's lunch status can be reevaluated," I told her with a smile.

She looked at me clearly upset. "I already filled one out and I am not going to fill out another one," she said, throwing the form on the desk. "This is another example of you not doing your job. You should be able to retrieve my original application."

"Ma'am, I do have your original application, but unfortunately your current income is too high to qualify for free lunch," I said.

"You mean to tell me that a single woman with kids can't get any financial support." Her tone went up a couple of decibels. "This is ridiculous. Take this money and give me a receipt!"

As soon as I wrote the receipt and handed it to her, she snatched it from my hand and stormed out of the office with these words, "I think I am going to give Mr. Banker a call."

What a piece of work, I thought, as I helped the next parent in line. Every person in the queue carried the same hostility into the office that day except for one, Ms. Winder. She had two daughters that attended the school and was a very active parent. She attended all the school functions and volunteered whenever we needed someone to help.

"How are you today, Mr. White?" she said cheerfully.

"Much better now that everyone is gone," I answered.

"Mr. White, I heard you were a big time consultant before coming to this school. Your wife must be mad at you for leaving the good life and coming here."

I shook my head. "No, she was okay with it. She knew why I wanted to do this."

"And why is that?" she asked.

"You know, I have been asking myself that same question lately," I chuckled. "I came because I could see potential. I believe that I can help make a change in this community."

"That's wishful thinking, Mr. White." She threw me a questioning gaze. "And do you think you have made a difference yet?"

"I don't know. It doesn't seem that way. This has been very eye opening for me though. For example, these parents were complaining about paying for meals for their children. However, they are willing to pay hundreds of dollars just so their child can go skating. They can take their kids skating on their own and only pay twenty. What kind of message are they sending to their kids?"

"That is the mentality of our community."

"That mentality is not going to cut it if they want to see more than just our community or improve it for that matter," I said. "Why are you here anyway, Ms. Winder, you don't owe any money?"

"I know. I just want to put some money on my account. I like to stay ahead since I have some extra money this month. Also, can you give me another lunch application? I lost my job."

"Of course…," I said, retrieving another form from the filing cabinet. "When did this happen?"

"About two months ago."

"I'm sorry to hear that." I shook my head again. "Keep your money. Give me a copy of your last paycheck so I can make your lunch application retroactive to the time your income actually changed."

"Thanks, Mr. White," she said with an embarrassed smile crossing her lips.

"Why didn't you tell me sooner?"

"Well, I thought I would have gotten another job by now, but as you can see I haven't."

"Listen, send me your resume," I suggested. "I know another parent who sends me job posts regularly. I can send her your information."

"I really do appreciate the help, Mr. White." A grateful smile replaced the confounded one. "I will send it to you as soon as I get home."

"No problem at all, Ms. Winder," I said.

"See, Mr. White, you have already made a difference," she uttered, still smiling, as she left the office. "You just don't see it yet."

As she was leaving, I could hear Vonte in the hallway pretending to cry and saying, "Daddy, why can't I have an apple?"

A few days later, the school was unusually quiet. There was a calmness that I had never felt. It was very serene, maybe too serene.

"Mr. White, Ms. Deeds said she needs to talk to you," Mrs. Robinson said as she rushed into the office.

"Okay, give me a few minutes," I said.

"I think you may want to go now," she countered with urgency.

"Is everything okay?"

"Did you have any problems with a student a few days ago?"

"I have problems with students every day," I said jokingly.

"Well, you may want to hurry to Ms. Deeds' office," she insisted. "Andre Carson is in her office with his mother."

As I walked to the principal's office, I was trying to think of my encounters with Andre. He was a pretty good student and had never given me any trouble. I had no idea what was about to happen. I arrived in Ms. Deeds' office to find her along with Andre and his angry mother.

"Hello, Mr. White, please have a seat," said Ms. Deeds. "Ms. Carson has brought to my attention an accusation Andre made against you."

59

I was starting to feel the heat. *I know this little boy is not trying to accuse me of sexually assaulting him,* I thought. *I've seen too many stories of teachers being accused of something like this. This is serious.*

"Andre says that you were angry with him one morning and choked him in the cafeteria," Ms. Deeds said.

"Wait a minute, I've never choked you," I said to Andre.

"Are you saying my son is lying?" Ms. Carson questioned.

"Yes, you did!" Andre shouted. "You said if I continued to act up, you were going to choke me. You then put your hands around my neck and squeezed."

"Wait a minute, when did this happen?" I asked.

"Remember when I asked you what you would do if I disobeyed you?" he answered. "You said you would choke me."

"Wait, I remember that. I was playing with you. Why would I try to choke you for real? We were all laughing when I said that."

"Ms. Carson, I have never had a problem with Andre," I explained. "I wouldn't have a reason to bring any harm to him. I was playing with him along with the other boys at his table. I think we need to ask some of them what happened. I am sure they will tell a different story."

I couldn't believe that I was being falsely accused of something so serious.

"I think for now let's call this a misunderstanding," Ms. Deeds said while looking at me. "I will talk to Mr. White further and explain the importance of not touching the students. Ms. Carson, I don't think this is as serious as we originally thought, so let's relax a little bit."

Oh, this is serious alright, I thought. *This little brat just accused me of something for which I could go to jail.* I had heard the horror stories of people being falsely accused, especially men.

I left Ms. Deeds' office extremely upset.

"Mr. White," someone called to me as I was returning to the front office.

As I turned I could see who it was. It was Mr. Banker. Mr. Boogeyman himself decided to visit the campus.

"Mr. White, how are you?" Mr. Banker asked me. His eyes reflected a certain air of curious attention, which I hadn't seen in him before that day.

"I am excellent," I replied.

Mr. Banker was a short guy. He stood about 5'6" and waddled at around 250lbs. He tried to be intimidating; however, I wasn't going to let him scare me.

"Mr. White, I received an interesting email from a parent that detailed a heated exchange you guys had over meal money owed. Are you aware of Ms. Russell?" he asked.

"Yes, I am aware of her," I replied. "But I wouldn't call our conversation a heated exchange."

"Well she says that you were very rude and even questioned her stated income. Is that true?"

"No, that's not true. She was rude, and I did not…"

"Mr. White, I need you to understand the community you serve," he cut-in rudely to explain. "The majority of the people in this community are in dire need of assistance. Because of no fault of their own, they need help. And I will not deny a single mother any type of financial assistance that would aid her child's progression. Do we understand each other, Mr. White?"

I think it's time to put this man back in his place, I thought. "Yes, I think I understand very well," I said as calmly as I didn't feel.

I felt less than a man when he walked away from me. First I was falsely accused by a student that I actually liked. Then, I was belittled by a man, who, under different circumstances, I would have chewed up and spit out. *Is this really for me,* I thought. I haven't even made it through the first semester and all of this has happened. The very people that I am trying to help are trying to throw me into the fire. *I don't need this job.* I was perfectly happy where I was. As I was walking back to the office, a young 5th grader came up to me.

"What's up, Mr. White?"

"Hey, Robert," I said, not really paying attention.

"Why do you work here, Mr. White?"

"What do you mean?" I asked, his question bringing me out of my reveries.

"I mean, you don't look like a teacher. You like a business man. You look like someone who would be running a company rather than just teaching."

"Well, Robert, I started teaching because I want to help young men like you own a business one day."

"That's what's up, I mean, that's good, Mr. White," he said, correcting himself. "See ya later."

Looking at him running down the hallway, I felt the tearing apart of my purpose for being in that school returning at a gallop. Was I sacrificing too much? Among hundreds of parents, Ms. Winder had seen the difference I was trying to make and the assistance I was attempting to provide to children and parents in somewhat equal measure. But, Ms. Winder was one among too many who didn't see the forest for the trees.

A few days had passed and I was beginning to feel a little better about what happened in Ms. Deeds' office. That afternoon she rushed into the office and uncharacteristically grabbed my hand.

"Mr. White, I need you to come with me to my office. I need to talk to you." When we reached her office, she closed the door and said, "Mr. Washington will be resigning effective immediately."

"What happened?" I asked.

"He basically came into the office and confessed that he had lied on his employment application. There is a question on the application that asks if you have ever been terminated by a previous employer. He decided not to answer it. Turns out he had been terminated from another school. Apparently, he was stirring up the pot at another school and they let him go. Our HR department was doing some routine checks and discovered his omission. Instead of allowing them to contact the other school, he chose to resign. I just need you to make sure he doesn't leave with any of the school's property." She grabbed her car keys from the desk, put her bag over her shoulder and brushed past me. "I have a family emergency, so I cannot stay and watch him."

Bells were ringing in my head. *Wake up; get out of bed, the witch is dead. The wicked witch is dead* is what I kept singing to myself. Supafly was finally going down.

"I will definitely make sure he returns all of the school's property," I said emphatically.

It took several hours after school for him to pack which ended in my bundling all the rest of his stuff for him – a task I enjoyed tremendously. I felt as if I was throwing out the garbage that had encumbered my life since I had set eyes on this guy. His misery and burdensome attitude had dragged my intentions of fair play down into a hell hole of vengeance and I was glad to be rid of that malignant tumor once and for all. "Be careful what you ask for," is what I wanted to say to him – but didn't – as he walked down the hall one last time. I could just hear the dying sound of Shaft music as he exited the building.

Now we had to find a replacement.

"I have a resume from a young woman that has recently graduated from school," Mrs. Robinson said, when I returned to the office the next morning. "We can bring her in as a teacher's assistant since she's not certified and doesn't have any experience."

Her name was Becky Gillis. She was a decent looking woman with a little Tomboy thing going.

When she arrived for the interview, Ms. Deeds asked Mrs. Robinson and me to handle it because she was going to be out of the office. We grilled her pretty well. We worked very well together and fed off of each other. Mrs. Gillis was average, but there was something that interested Mrs. Robinson and me.

"I think she will be a hard worker and will listen well," Mrs. Robinson said after the interview.

"I agree," I replied. "She seems to have a good work ethic."

"I really like her." And Mrs. Robinson was very hard to please.

"I do too," I said. "I think we should give her a try."

Mrs. Gillis turned out to be a natural. She jumped right in and took over Mr. Washington's class without a hitch. The kids really liked her and actually respected her. She and Mrs. Robinson hit it off really well. They even started hanging out on the weekends. They acted like two childhood friends. Big Rob and Little Rob is what I named them.

Mr. Goodman came into the office one morning with a big smile on his face. "Good morning, Mr. White," he said happily.

"You seem to be in good spirits," I replied.

"Who is that young, pretty teacher you guys have hired?"

"Oh, that's Mrs. Gillis. She just started a couple of weeks ago."

"Well, she sure is fine."

"She's also married," I laughed.

"Oh, I don't want a young lady like that," he joked. "She would kill me. Besides, my wife would probably kill me first. Hey, I have quite a bit of candy money I need to give you, Mr. White. How do you want to handle it?"

"Good question. We don't have a safe, so I guess we can lock it in my cabinet. How much is it?"

"Oh, about eight thousand dollars," he said simply.

"Whoa, I guess I need to get that to the bank. I need to get with Mrs. Robinson and find out what the process is."

"Okay, don't forget, I trust you, Mr. White." Those were not empty words – he needed to trust me entirely with that amount of money.

"I understand, Mr. Goodman," I said. "I will make sure this gets deposited."

I don't know when I will be able to do it, I thought. *I never have any real down time. Besides Ms. Deeds has been out a lot lately and Mrs. Robinson has to go to meetings all the time. I will just lock it up for now.*

Mrs. Robinson walked in as Mr. Goodman was exiting.

"Hello, Mr. Goodman," she said.

"Hi," he replied. "See ya later, Mr. White."

"Mr. White, I'm going to Pappadeaux's for lunch," Mrs. Robinson said. "Do you want anything?"

"Man, you guys are rich around here," I joked. "No, I don't have that kind of money today."

"Don't worry about it. I got it," she offered.

"Uh, okay, I will pay next time," I said, surprised. "By the way, Mrs. Robinson, Mr. Goodman just dropped off a ton of candy money. What's the procedure for making the deposits?"

"Just fill out the deposit slip and send a copy to accounting," she said. "Also, leave us about $200 for miscellaneous expenses."

"Do we have a cash register or safe?"

"No, keep it in your desk, if you don't mind."

"So when do you normally make deposits?"

"Whenever you have some down time."

When is that, I thought. *If I leave, no one will be in the office.*

"Okay," I said. "Oh, before I forget, Ms. Berry wants to meet with Ms. Deeds Friday to discuss Alicia's suspension."

"That won't happen," she replied matter-of-factly. "Ms. Deeds and Mr. Jackson are going to New Orleans to visit one of our charter schools from Thursday through Monday."

"Mr. Jackson…? Why is he going?" I asked.

"Good question," she said. "He is supposed to be on the fast track to leadership, so Ms. Deeds is trying to get his name out there. I don't know why. He's not that good of a teacher and I personally don't trust him. He seems shady to me."

"Man, you are a hard woman to please," I said, chuckling. "You don't like Mr. Jackson, Ms. Ebony, and Ms. Lloyd. Am I missing someone?"

"Yes," she replied. "Don't forget about you."

We both laughed.

"I don't like Ms. Ebony and Ms. Lloyd because they take advantage of their friendship with Ms. Deeds," she said. "Ms. Ebony is always sick or drunk and Ms. Lloyd complains too much. Ms. Lloyd is a teacher's assistant with no degree, makes almost as much as the teachers and still complains. Ms. Ebony gets paid almost as much as Ms. Deeds because she is the assistant principal, but how often do you see her actually performing those duties? Hell, you have met with more parents than she has, Mr. White."

Well, I can't argue with that, I thought.

"To top it all off, Ms. Lloyd's daughter is trying to get a job here," Mrs. Robinson went on. "I can't have anyone else in that family working here. Have you seen her daughter? She looks like a crack addict and acts like one too. Mr. White, it's our job to make sure this school is run the right way. Ms. Deeds can be a pushover at times and if I have to be the hammer, I will be that. This school has to succeed."

A reluctant coach

I was never able to make the deposit that day. Before I knew it, it was time for dismissal. Just as I was leaving, Coach Robinson approached me.

"What's up, White," he said. "You have a minute?"

"Yeah, what's up?"

"I couldn't find another coach for basketball," he stated. "I know you said you don't want to do it, but the kids really need someone they trust."

"What about Coach Steel?"

"The boys don't like him. He gets too rough with them. I constantly have to talk with him about putting his hands on the kids, so I know if I let him coach something bad will happen."

"Okay, let me talk to my wife about it and I will let you know. When do you need an answer?"

"Well, we have our first practice tomorrow and the first game in one week."

"Damn, you didn't try to find another coach, did you?"

"I did, but your name kept coming up," he said.

"Okay, you got me, but if my wife gets mad, it's your fault!"

News traveled quickly that I was going to coach the basketball team. The question they all wanted to know was can I even play. The kids had never seen me do anything athletic which was by design. I knew my lane at the school. I didn't want to be viewed as a coach, we had two of those. I wasn't the young, up-and-coming guy. That was Mr. Jackson. And I wasn't the father figure type. That was Mr. Anderson. I wanted the kids to see a corporate image. An image most of them had never really seen. So I dressed in button down shirts and slacks every day, even on Fridays, which was supposed to be dress down day.

Since our school was located in a church, the basketball court was not in a real gym. The cafeteria doubled as the auditorium, detention center and, on Sundays, a sanctuary for church service. It was small, but we did have two basketball goals.

Approximately thirty boys showed up for tryouts that evening. I intentionally came late so that I could make my grand entrance. When I walked through the doors I could sense the stares. They had never seen me in Nikes, warm-up pants and a muscle shirt. The first thing I did was place several cones on the floor.

"I want you to dribble to each cone, reverse spin and make a left hand lay-up," I shouted, after placing the cones. "Give me two lines."

They hesitantly lined up and tried the drill. These were 7th graders who believed they knew how to play, and running through the cones was nothing. Not one kid could make it to the opposite end without messing up.

"Throw me a ball," I said. "Let me show you how to do it."

I ran through those cones effortlessly while shouting out how I was doing it, ending with a left handed finger roll. You could have heard a pin drop. They were shocked that I could even dribble the ball. I think I got their attention. Any questioning of my ability came to an end. Coach Robinson and Mrs. Gillis had the biggest smiles on their faces as they watched from the sideline.

"Now, we are going to do a passing drill we call the weave," I shouted to the boys' astounded faces. "I need three volunteers."

No one would raise a hand, so I picked the three boys whom I thought may have been the top players.

"You will start at this end of the court in three lines, one in the middle and one near each sideline," I explained. "The first person in the middle line starts the weave by passing to one of the sideline players. He then cuts wide around and behind the player he passed the ball to. That player now passes to the opposite sideline player and cuts around and behind him. Now the player with the ball passes to the original middle person and cuts around him. And so it goes on and on until you reach the other basket. You cannot dribble except to finish with a lay-up. The ball should never touch the floor unless it is the last pass to the shooter. Does everyone understand?" I asked, even though I knew they didn't.

"Yes, sir," they shouted.

The first group tried it, but couldn't make it past the second pass without messing up.

"Get off the court!" I yelled. "Give me another group!"

Those kids were running like chickens with their heads cut off. This is a tough drill for anyone, if you have never seen it before. I knew they would struggle with it and I enjoyed it.

"Okay, kids, let me show you how it's done," I uttered with unabated pride. "Coach Robinson, Mrs. Gillis and I are going to run this drill twice without the ball touching the floor."

I knew they could do it, because they both played basketball before. We ran it like clockwork and I talked to the kids the whole time I was doing it. The ball never touched the ground. We ran down and back twice and then I substituted Coach and Mrs. Gillis with two kids I thought could run with me. Up and down we ran. Each time back I would substitute two more. We did this until everyone had an opportunity to go through the drill. Everything was fast paced. I didn't even stop between substitutions. When they would mess up, I would replace them. They hated that. As a result, they tried their best not to make mistakes. We were about 30 minutes into practice and the kids were concentrating more than I had ever seen them. This was a way to reach the majority of them.

One kid, Stanley, was extremely overweight and having trouble keeping up.

"Why are you in here, Stanley?" I asked.

"Because I want to play basketball," he answered timidly.

"You're too big, Stanley. You need to play football not basketball."

"I know, sir, that's not the only reason I'm out here. My momma wants me to lose weight."

"Well, Stanley, if you don't quit, I will make sure you lose the weight," I said. "So, get your butt on the line and let's run. As a matter of fact, everyone get on the line. It's time to run."

This was the part of practice I hated as a child, running sprints. I had a coach that made us run until we would literally cry. However, we were always in tip top shape. I was a little concerned though, because the kids these days were dropping like flies and those old school tactics were not smiled upon. So I decided to run with them. If I couldn't do it, then I wouldn't push them too hard was what I thought. We ran and ran. By this time parents were in the gym watching and they could feel the intensity. It was an unbelievable first practice. When practice ended, the kids didn't call me Mr. White. They called me Coach. I had now been upgraded in their eyes. I could feel the level of respect from them rise. It was ironic, because that was a title that I didn't want, but now appreciated. *Well, if being a coach will allow me to reach these kids, then so be it,* I thought.

I made the kids wear shirts and ties on game days, which they didn't really like. The teachers loved it. They were getting compliments the entire day.

71

"Looking good in that suit, Mr. White," Ms. Trout said one day.

"Thank you," I replied.

I wanted the boys to carry themselves with more pride. "When you look good, you feel good" is what I told them. Our first game was a pushover. We won by thirty points and the parents were really excited. Several fathers were coming out and wanting to give their input. I knew in their eyes I was still not an adequate coach, because I didn't fit the mold. They didn't know my basketball background. They didn't see me run through those drills like their sons did, so they thought they knew best. *No worries,* I thought, *I will show them.*

This time there was no high school coach to slow me down or stop me. I finally felt as if I could make a difference – the kids were listening to me and they were absorbing my words like sponges. It felt good being able to shed my "reluctant coach" attitude for the pleasure of seeing the children finally admiring something other than rudeness and ignorant behavior.

Our second game was a real nail biter. We were playing a catholic school that was well coached. Everything they did was like clockwork. Three crisp passes and a lay-up was their style of play. Unfortunately, my boys still didn't fully believe in what I was telling them. So when the game was nearing the final buzzer, they reverted back to their old ways. Each time out I called, I would try to reinforce the idea of believing in their teammates and in what I was telling them. Unfortunately, they still didn't believe. With five seconds to go and down by three, I called my final timeout. I drew up a simple play for the boys that would tie the score.

"Listen," I said calmly. "Believe me, if you run the play correctly, Percy will have an open look at the three."

The timeout ended and they returned to the floor and began getting in their positions. They were running the play exactly how I drew it up.

However, instead of going left the way I showed him, Percy decided to go right, which was exactly where the defense thought he was going. He was able to get the shot off, but it was not even close. The buzzer went off and we lost our first game. The boys were crushed.

Our next game started out as a laugher. We had gotten ahead by as much as 20 points. However, the other team started to chip away at our lead. Just like in the last game, my boys started to revert to old, bad habits. Before we knew it, we were losing the game. I was shocked and frustrated, and they were as well. We lost by ten points which made for a long bus ride home. There was no need to scold them; they did that very well on their own. Yet, I noticed that some of the boys began recognizing that every time they reverted to their old ways, we began to lose. The next practice turned out to be as grueling as I had ever seen it. Winning at everything was in their make-up, and losing a game – just a game – meant losing face, losing self-confidence and the respect they had earned from the other kids since they had begun playing competitively. In short, their hatred for losing translated in intense practices, where every boy became as vicious as if their lives depended on "winning". As for me, I had only one thought in mind; *I can't lose the next game. If we lose again, I may lose them.*

Just before the next game, Coach Robinson came to me with some disturbing news.

"White, the team I originally scheduled you to play canceled on us," he said. "However, I was able to find a replacement."

"Okay, that's good. Who are they?" I asked.

"Well...." He paused. "It's Boys and Girls Prep."

"Wait a minute, aren't they 9th and 10th graders?"

73

"Yes, they are, but they are a new school," he rationalized. "That means they don't have too many students that really play well."

"There is a big difference between inexperienced 7th graders and 10th graders who are bigger and stronger." I looked at his face. He wanted for us to play. So there was no alternative. "Okay, so we won't tell the boys how old they really are."

When we arrived into the gym I could see my boys' eyes get really big. They could not believe how big these middle school kids were.

"What's wrong, gentlemen?" I chided. "I know you are not scared. Look at them. They are a bunch of big, slow guys. We can run them all day."

Unfortunately, they didn't quite believe me.

Ironically, they were a bunch of big, slow kids. However, their star player was not. He ran us out of the gym. He made three pointers with ease. On rare occasions when he missed, he would get the rebound and put it right back in. They were beating us by 20 up until the 4th quarter.

"Well, gentlemen, if you just listen to what I am telling you we can get back in this game," I said. "Believe me; we can get back into this."

The next few plays we ran worked like a charm. We actually started to chip away at their lead. Before we knew it, the lead had been reduced to 10 points with a few minutes to play. The kids were excited. The parents were starting to feel the buzz. Unfortunately, the other team's star player could feel it too. He turned it up a notch and took over the game again. We lost the game by 13 points, but I could sense a change in my boys. When we got on the bus to go home I let them in on a little secret.

"Just so you all know, we just lost to a high school team," I said. "You were able to compete on a high school level and didn't even know it. You were able to compete because you believed in yourselves."

"I knew it," Charles exclaimed.

"They were much bigger than us," Andre said.

"We could've beaten them," said Leonard who didn't even play.

"Yeah, we could have beaten them…," they all began to repeat.

"We need to play them again, Coach," Kendrick said. "We will beat them next time."

I just want to stop losing, I thought. We continued our terrible streak by losing the next two games. Our record was 1 win and 5 losses. It wasn't looking too good, but amazingly the boys never got down on themselves. I kept preaching the concept of "believing in oneself", but I was starting not to believe in myself.

Our next game was against another middle school that just happened to be undefeated. They had two kids who were really good. One was a small, quick point guard and the other was a tall, skinny kid who played like Kobe Bryant. Before the game started we had our usual pep talk.

"Listen, guys, tonight is the night we right the ship," I said. "This team has not won a game. We can't lose to them. I don't want to be the team they get their first win against. We have to show some pride and pull this one out."

They believed it. Besides, they didn't want to be embarrassed. My boys played unbelievably well. The two stars of the other team were bickering and arguing the entire game. We won by twenty points and I could not have been more ecstatic.

Thank God, thank God for this victory, I thought. The bus ride home was great, but I had to let them in on my little secret.

"Good win, gentlemen," I said. "You won that game because you believed you could win. What you didn't know was that team was undefeated. You beat a team that had not lost a game, because you believed in each other. Good victory."

This was getting serious

I was starting to like this coaching thing, but it was tiresome.

"Mr. White, good win the other day," said Mrs. Robinson.

"Thanks, we sure needed it," I replied.

"I hope you haven't forgotten, but our teacher retreat is coming up."

"I haven't forgotten," I said, even though I really had.

Things had been so hectic that I have been forgetting a lot lately. *I think I just need a break. I can't wait until Christmas vacation comes*, I thought.

"I will be out of the office most of the week so I can make sure everything is set for the retreat. You can call me if you need anything. Also, Ms. Berry is coming in today to talk about Alicia. You may have to conference with her."

"Conference with her about what?" I asked.

"Just tell her that Alicia has run out of chances and she needs to withdraw her or face expulsion."

"Got it."

"See you later," she said, as she walked out.

As expected, Ms. Berry arrived into the office right after Mrs. Robinson left.

"I need to speak with Ms. Deeds," she demanded.

"I'm sorry, Ms. Berry, she isn't in the office, but she did ask me to speak with you," I replied kindly but firmly.

"Why do I need to speak with you? You don't make any decisions around here."

"Well, Ms. Berry, Ms. Deeds instructed me to advise you to find another school for Alicia," I relayed.

"What!" she screamed.

"Ms. Berry, Alicia has repeatedly shown us that she will not abide by the rules of this school. Therefore, we are advising you to withdraw your daughter or face expulsion."

"What, expulsion!" Her voice carried all the way down the hallway this time. "I spoke with Ms. Deeds on the phone this morning and she didn't say anything about this. She told me that Alicia was doing better and that she just needed more time. Now you tell me this. Maybe you need to call Ms. Deeds and clear all this up, because Alicia is not going anywhere."

Just as I was about to address her statement, we could hear Ms. Deeds in the hallway speaking on her cell phone. She walked in, motioned to Mrs. Berry to follow her and left. I didn't know what to think. I wondered if she really spoke with Ms. Deeds. Did she really say that Alicia was doing better? Alicia seemed to be getting worse to me. She averaged at least one fight a week and was only suspended once. Just as I got over that confrontation, Mr. Goodman walked in.

"Mr. White, we need to talk," he said sternly. "You said that I could trust you. Why haven't you deposited the money I gave you?"

Damn, I thought. *I forgot all about the money. I hope it's still locked in the cabinet.*

"I'm sorry, Mr. Goodman. I just haven't had time to do it."

"It's been a few weeks, Mr. White, and I have more money to give you," he said. "However, I don't want to give it to you if you are not going to deposit it."

"I understand, I really do," I replied. "I can assure you the money is still here. Let me show you."

I hope this money is in this cabinet, I thought as we stepped to it.

"You see, it's still here," I said with a sigh of relief. "I just can't leave the office without any coverage, Mr. Goodman, and the banks close before I leave work."

"Alright, Mr. White, here is seven thousand more. Please deposit the money." His visible anxiety was understandable. "I would hate to hear someone stole it."

"I will make sure this gets deposited, Mr. Goodman," I said, not knowing how I was going to do it.

"Alright, Mr. White, I hope you do or we may need to talk with Mr. Banker." That's when my smile turned into a stern frown. *Don't threaten me with Mr. Banker,* I thought. I couldn't care less what he thinks. *I don't bow down to him like everyone else.* At that moment my relationship with Mr. Goodman changed.

If I had to jot down my thoughts at the conclusion of that day, they would have read something like this:

I need some help in this office. I have too much to do and no time to do it. I can't get the attendance out on time, because I have to help serve breakfast. Then I have to monitor classes because teachers show up late or don't show up at all. I can't work on balancing the budget because I have to help with lunch. When I am not doing that, I am conferencing with parents about their bad kids. I have to stop what I am doing every five minutes to deal with kids that are sent to the office for just about anything. Then I spend my evenings with the basketball team. I miss my wife. I miss my daughter. I miss my life. I need some help.

When the opportunity presented itself and Mrs. Robinson and I were alone in the office, I asked her, "Do you think we can hire someone to help out in the office?"

"I think so," she replied. "We need someone desperately. Do you have anyone in mind?"

"No, but we need someone like Mrs. Gillis," I suggested.

"I have a friend that referred someone to me a long time ago. I'll give him a call today."

A few days later Mr. Howard showed up. He was a tall, energetic guy. I could tell he was eager to impress and really wanted to teach. I interviewed him and he did very well. I was really impressed with his energy and tenacity. He was real big on brotherhood and belonging to something. Mrs. Robinson interviewed him as well and suggested we give him a try.

He started working right away which surprised me, given that he did have another job. For two weeks, he worked with us during the day and continued working at his previous job at night. After his two week notice ended, his obligation to his previous employer was over. He started off pretty well. He was very organized and listened to instruction. He was a real sparkplug, almost to a fault. You could tell when he was overly excited, because his voice would get louder and his pitch would get much higher.

"Good morning, boss," he would say to me with a heavy southern accent.

One morning before school had begun, Mrs. Robinson rushed into the office, "Mr. White, we need to talk in Ms. Deeds' office," she blurted.

Ms. Deeds was already in her office waiting for us when we arrived.

"Hey, Mr. White," Ms. Deeds said. "How are you?"

"You look nice today," I said.

"Thanks, I feel great. I'm not sick anymore. My mother is doing better. I'm single – but not officially. I feel great." She paused and opened the file in front of her. "Listen, we have a problem with Mr. Howard. Human Resources did a background check and he has some felonies on his record. We can't have felons working here."

"So what can we do?" I asked. "He has been here for a few weeks and he quit his previous job."

"Well, Mr. Banker said he has to leave the campus immediately." Ms. Deeds sounded as adamant as Banker would have been, if he had attended the meeting. "I have already spoken with Mr. Howard and he said that those charges are not accurate. He claims he received a traffic ticket that was miscoded and that he has been trying to clear this up for some time now. I told HR to look further into it, but as of now he has to leave. So, Mrs. Robinson, go ahead and relieve him of his duties and tell him I will give him a call."

"No problem," Mrs. Robinson replied, getting to her feet, turning on her heels and leaving her office.

Damn, I thought, *no more help.* I was about to get up when Ms. Deeds recalled me to attention.

"Mr. White, I may need you to go back into the classroom as well," she said, muttering the words as if she was not agreeing with the suggestion.

"Okay, what happened?" I asked a little more than stunned.

"I don't think Mr. Gordon is going to work out." She fixed her gaze on me. "It seems that he isn't teaching the kids anything. They just read their textbooks every day."

"I thought Mr. Gordon was doing well. Do you mind if I have a talk with him?"

"No, not at all, Mr. White. He's a good guy, and believe me, I don't want to get rid of him just like that."

"Okay, give him some time. I will talk with him this afternoon," I said.

Just as we were finishing, a parent walked into Ms. Deeds' office.

"Oh, I'm sorry," the lady said. "I didn't realize someone was in here with you."

"No, come in, Ms. Giles, it's just White," Ms. Deeds said. "He's cool."

Ms. Giles glanced at me and then proceeded to pull three boxes of birth control pills out of her bag.

"I recommend you use this one and then this one," she said.

"Okay, thanks. You know I ain't trying to have any more babies," Ms. Deeds said, throwing a wink and a smile in my direction.

What the hell is going on here, I wondered. Why do you have a parent bringing you birth control is what I wanted to ask. And why does everyone know about your impending divorce. I thought she was sharing something confidential when she told me. *I don't want to be a part of this,* I thought.

"Okay, Ms. Deeds, I need to get back to the office," I said.

"Okay. Tell Mrs. Robinson to let me know how her conversation with Mr. Howard went."

Wait until I tell Regina about this, I thought as I walked back to the office. Mr. Howard was just leaving as I was entering.

"Keep your head up," I said. "I am sure everything will work out just fine."

"I hope so," he replied. "I have bills to pay. As of right now, I can't pay them if I don't have a job."

"Well, you should receive a check for the time that you have been here," I said.

"I don't know, Mr. White. Ms. Deeds seemed to imply that I wouldn't. She said she would pay me out of her pocket if need be."

"Why wouldn't they pay you?" I asked.

"She said HR is accusing me of lying on my application and technically I was never hired."

"Don't worry. Ms. Deeds will work something out." I was trying to uplift his spirit.

"I hope so," he muttered as he walked out of the office.

Mrs. Robinson looked at me. "I hate for him to go through this."

"I am starting to notice a pattern here. Things aren't too stable around here are they?" I asked her.

Keeping her eyes on me, she went on, "It is more unstable than you think, Mr. White. Anyway, I need to go to a meeting and will be back in a few hours. Don't forget to send out reminders for the retreat. It's only a few weeks away."

"Okay, I will send them out now," I replied.

That evening the basketball practice went really well. The boys were listening and believing in every word I was saying. I could feel the difference one win made.

"Have you lost any weight, Stanley?" I asked.

"Yes, sir," he replied with a broad grin on his face.

"Good, I need five shirts and five skins on the court," I yelled. We were about to play a scrimmage. "Stanley, you are with the skins," I told him.

Stanley gave me a look that was priceless. I needed him to gain some confidence without crushing him. He paused for a moment contemplating what he was going to do. He didn't want to remove his shirt, but he didn't want to miss out on an opportunity to play either.

"Hurry up, Stanley," shouted Scooter, my little fearless point guard.

Stanley took his shirt off and joined the rest of the players on the court. No one snickered. No hurtful comments were made. I could see the relief

Stanley was feeling. My plan worked. Stanley hustled and made plays that I didn't think he could make.

"Stanley came to play today," I shouted enthusiastically as I hit him on the butt.

"I am really proud of you all," I told the boys. "I can see each one of you changing. You are in this together and believe in each other. This is what is meant by team. You have to be this way on and off the court. The tools you learn in this gym will help you in everyday life. Good practice, gentlemen. We have a game tomorrow, so let's get some rest and let's get another win."

Mrs. Robinson and Mrs. Gillis came into the gym laughing hysterically after the boys left.

"Mr. White, you know you were wrong for having Stanley take his shirt off," Mrs. Robinson laughed.

"His chest is bigger than mine," Mrs. Gillis said as they both giggled.

"Hey, lay off my boy, he played his butt off today," I said with a smile. "Besides, my chest is bigger than both of you."

"That's alright, our husbands like them," Mrs. Robinson said sassily.

"That's right. What we lack in the front, we make up for in the back," Mrs. Gillis rejoined. They both laughed and walked out of the gym purposely twisting hard like young school girls.

Our next game went according to plan. The boys played up to their potential and we won easily.

"Congratulations on the victory last night," said Mr. Gordon.

"Thanks, I appreciate it," I replied. "Hey, do you have a minute?"

"Yes, what's up?"

"How are things going with the kids? Are you starting to settle in?" I asked.

Mr. Gordon paused before he answered and gave me a peculiar look. I could tell he was trying to read me.

"I am asking because I want to make sure you have all the help you need. I don't want you to feel like you are on an island alone."

"Everything is okay, I guess," he said with a smile. "Honestly, these are some of the most disrespectful kids that I have ever been around. I came from an alternative high school with kids that were capable of doing some really bad things, but they weren't this disrespectful."

"Mr. Gordon, I am asking this because this is my first time working in a school. Are you saying that most schools are not like this?"

"No!" he said emphatically. "I have had students steal my lunch, openly use profanity and refuse to abide by any of my rules."

"Whoa," I said. "Did you tell Ms. Deeds?"

"I sure did. She told me to get with my grade level chair, Mr. Anderson. But Mr. Anderson hasn't done anything either. Mr. Anderson or "Mr. Perfect" is too busy criticizing my teaching ability and classroom management."

"You're having problems with Mr. Anderson?" I asked surprised.

"He is critical of everything I do, but I see the same things happening in his class. He tells me not to yell at the students, but I can hear him screaming all the time. He kicks kids out of class and tells me I should not put them out because of safety issues."

I could see the anger and frustration in Mr. Gordon's face as he was talking. "I had no idea you were going through all of this," I said.

"Oh yeah, and then some. Ms. Deeds has been telling people that she is going to let me go as well. She put me on an improvement plan, so I know what the next step is."

"Let's not jump the gun," I said. "Let me help you. I can speak with Ms. Deeds and try to smooth some of this over. Do you mind if I do that?"

"Actually, I would prefer that you didn't. I have tried talking to her on several occasions, but it's obvious that she is not interested in my success. I am just going to finish out the year and move on."

"Okay, I won't say a word. But I really hope you change your mind. Even though I agree that most of these kids are difficult, they need to see more men like you. Just maybe they will realize what a good resource you are."

Mr. Gordon shook his head in disgust as he went to his classroom. "See ya later, White."

Why didn't Ms. Deeds tell me what Mr. Gordon had been going through? What's the deal? I need to speak with Mr. Anderson. We have a pretty good relationship, so I think he will tell me what's going on. Meanwhile, I better get to the cafeteria. It's lunch time.

When I arrived, the kids were being their usual bad selves. I suppose this was the straw that broke the camel's back. After my conversation with Mr. Gordon, my kettle didn't only flip its lid but my "cup runneth over."

"SIT DOWN AND SHUT UP!" I yelled as I entered the cafeteria. My voice resonated from every eave above my head.

The kids weren't accustomed to me yelling and showing real anger.

"I DON'T WANT TO HEAR ONE VOICE IN THIS ROOM!" I shouted as I slammed my clipboard on the table.

It was dead silence, but as usual someone decided to test my patience. Vonte decided to let out a chuckle, so the kids around him began to laugh. *Not today,* I thought. I couldn't get to his side of the room fast enough. I shoved tables and chairs out of my path as I made my way to him. I tried to make it as dramatic and scary as possible. The other kids were stunned and so was Vonte.

"Do you think I'm playing with you?" I said. "Huh, answer me! Say something else. I dare you!"

He didn't say anything, but I could see his heart beating through his chest.

"Go stand against the wall," I yelled.

He looked at me as though he was not going to do it, so I gave him a look that my father used to give me. The look that meant I was about to receive a serious beat down. Vonte knew what the look meant as well. He picked up his things and stood by the wall.

"Does anyone else want to try me?" I yelled. "I didn't think so. We are going to sit here until I decide it's time to eat."

I could hear the moans and groans, but they remained silent. Holding back lunch was one way to get the kids to act properly. I really felt bad for the good kids, because they weren't doing anything to deserve this.

Once they had settled down and I saw that some degree of respect for the school's authority as a whole had been re-established, I allowed the good kids to eat first while I let the others sweat it out.

I need a vacation

It was now November and the teacher retreat was upon us. Our entire staff went out to this country resort just outside of the city for a weekend getaway of bonding and seminars. The lodge was a well-appointed, very large log cabin, standing tall atop a plateau overlooking a small but refreshing pond. We were surrounded by a luxuriant spread of trees. We each had our own room, some of them looking over the pond while mine was looking onto the forest at the back of the building. It was a perfect location for me to reflect on the months that I had spent in the school thus far. Had I made a difference? In some ways – very small ways mind you – I had. In others, I had been incapable of mastering the art of managing these children or giving them enough desire to learn something. Notwithstanding the fact that some of their lives had been plagued with problems most adults shouldn't even encounter, they didn't have, it seemed, any desire or innate want for exploring the possibilities or opportunities that the school would offer them in the long run. The barriers they had erected before them seemed to be indestructible. These shields were not only protecting them from the hurt and shame but they were preventing them from going out into the world that was at their doorstep. It seemed to me that they had persuaded themselves long ago – probably since birth – that their condition or situation was to be their irreversible destiny.

Coming out of my self-examination, on that first night, I went to meet the teachers and staff from another all boys' charter school we had partnered with. Their school leader was a real character. His name was

Juan Hart. He was extremely loud and made sure everyone knew he was in the room. He reminded me of an opera singer when he spoke, because he was very theatrical and demonstrative. He also had this metro sexual thing going, which I began noticing was a common theme.

We were on the retreat for three days and two nights. Our days were filled with seminars centered on self-growth and improvement. Our nights were very care free and laid-back – almost too laid-back if you asked me. Mr. Howard had been invited to the retreat as well. Ms. Deeds wanted him not to feel excluded and still part of the team even though he had not officially been hired yet. This was his opportunity to really show his worth. Unfortunately for him, he started to show signs of someone we should think twice about hiring.

The first night we were all in Coach Robinson's room which had become the hangout. Mr. Howard arrived with his fake diamond earrings and pants sagging down to his knees with his boxers showing.

"Where da party at?" he yelled as he came through the door.

No one really paid much attention to him, but I did. He would laugh at everything as if it were the funniest joke he had ever heard while repeatedly grabbing his crotch.

Doesn't this fool realize he is still amongst co-workers, I wondered. However, no one really seemed to mind. People were playing cards or dominos and drinking the alcohol that had been purchased for the occasion. *Maybe I'm just being a little too stiff,* I thought. *Or maybe I just need to get some sleep.* I retired early that night, but I knew the night was just beginning for most of them.

The next morning everyone met in the dining room for breakfast. I could tell most of them had partied pretty hard the previous night.

"Man, you missed it, Mr. White," said Mr. Steel. "It got pretty wild."

"I can only imagine," I replied, raising one quizzical eyebrow.

One of the perks of the retreat was the free massages. We were all given complimentary hour long massages. There was a woman masseuse for the men and two men masseurs available for the women. We were all given a specific time slot so we didn't have to worry about waiting. Fortunately for me my time slot was pretty early. However, a lot of people had to wait up late for theirs.

"Did you hear about Mr. Hart last night?" Mr. Steel asked.

"No, what did he do?" I asked in turn.

"Well, it seems he didn't want to wait for his turn with the female masseuse," Mr. Steel chuckled. "Mr. Hart took one of the women's slots and received a massage from one of the men."

"Is that right? To each his own, I suppose."

For the rest of that day, we focused on how to teach. We ended with a discussion on why we were here. Why did we want to work for a charter school? Why did we want to spend countless hours in a profession that was under-appreciated?

"Why are you here, Mr. White?" Mr. Hart asked.

"I'm here because my spirit led me here," I responded, even though it was a question I was beginning to wrestle with. "I am here because my community needs me and I need my community. I can't continue to sit on the sidelines and watch this game in which we're all supposed to play a part. The only way I can see a different result is if I do something. I must be involved or else I am really a part of the problem. I am here because I am supposed to be here."

I left the retreat with a renewed sense of purpose. I felt much better about my decision to join the school.

I returned to school that Monday revitalized and ready to make change. However, the kids quickly reminded me who was actually running the school.

I was in the cafeteria monitoring the kids while they ate breakfast. There was a routine that the kids were supposed to follow every morning. They were to pick up a worksheet as they entered the cafeteria and work on it while they ate their breakfast. However, the kids never completed the work because they knew it was not going to be graded, even though they were constantly told the opposite.

This particular morning I just wanted to observe the kids. Most of them were actually doing what they were supposed to be doing. Unfortunately, a good number of them were not. Some students were texting on their phones that they were not supposed to have. Some of them were listening to their MP3 players, which was against the rules. Then there was a group of students who decided to just yell and scream. They took turns screaming words like "Stop" or "Hey" just for kicks. There was one girl in particular who really went overboard. She would intentionally speak with a loud, nasal tone. She spoke like Fran Drescher from the "*Nanny*" on steroids. She just kept laughing for no reason and it was starting to get to me. Just as I was about to say something to her, Mr. Jackson rushed up to me.

"Mr. White, I really need to speak with you," he said with a sense of urgency.

"Sure," I said, "what's up?"

"Can I tell you something in strict confidence?"

I could sense the seriousness in his voice. "Definitely."

"I am having some trouble with Ms. Deeds. She is going to suspend me for insubordination."

"What did you do?" I asked.

"She said that I haven't been returning her calls, and because I called-in sick one day last week."

I was thinking two things. We can't afford to have any teachers out since we don't use substitute teachers. Second, I know there are other teachers doing far worse things.

"Are you sure those are the reasons she gave for a suspension?" I asked.

"Those are the reasons she stated, but I know the real reason," he said. "She's upset because I don't want to be involved with her any longer."

Whoa, I thought. *I wasn't expecting to hear that.*

"Mr. White, she propositioned me. We were in her office late one night and she came on to me. She told me that she was going to divorce her husband and she was only looking for a physical relationship. Honestly, I thought it was an ideal situation for me. I thought since she was older she would be more mature, but I was wrong. I don't want to be in a committed relationship. I am young, and besides she's still married."

"Well, Mr. Jackson, I have to say the rumors were starting to grow," I remarked. "I was hoping that they weren't true. This is not good. You can't sleep with your boss. Do you realize that she can ruin your career?"

"I know," he said. "I talked it over with my family and they suggested I try to get with another school."

"Your family knows about this?" I asked, taken aback.

"Yes, we have been messing around for quite some time, so my mother and siblings have seen her at my house."

"First of all let me say I appreciate that you think I am trustworthy, so I won't tell anyone about this. I think you need to start documenting everything. At this point she can paint a really bad picture of you if she wants. You don't want anything negative to go on your record if you want to continue teaching. I also think you should start looking for another school. I suggest you immediately have a talk with her and try to smooth things over so she doesn't get any angrier than she already is."

"You're right. I knew I could get some sound advice from you, Mr. White, since you are much, much older," he joked. "Thanks for listening and for the advice. But, for now, I need to get to my classroom before the kids come."

What the hell is going on around here, I thought. Just when I was feeling rejuvenated; something happened that just took all the wind out of my sails. I was pretty much in a trance for the rest of the day. I really wanted to believe in Ms. Deeds. I really wanted to see her succeed. I didn't want to believe that this was the stereotypical charter school. On the other hand, how could I trust Mr. Jackson? I did believe there was some sort of relationship, but what if he was trying to set her up? He could be trying to position himself to take her job. Or, he may be attempting to blackmail her so she could never get rid of him. *I don't know what to think.*

"Mr. White, Mr. White!" I could hear someone yelling my name. Melissa, a sixth grader, frantically ran into the office. "Mr. White, something is wrong with Ms. Gibbons!" she said between gasps.

"Okay, calm down and speak slowly," I suggested.

"Ms. Gibbons is in the restroom and she doesn't look good. Something is really wrong. There is vomit all over the place."

We rushed to the restroom and I could hear her moaning faintly.

"Are you okay, Ms. Gibbons?" I asked from the doorway.

Just as I was about to go in, Mrs. Robinson came rushing in. She took one look into the stall and said, "Call 911 immediately!"

The ambulance arrived within minutes. It turned out that Ms. Gibbons was severely dehydrated. Since she was too weak to walk the EMTs had to take her out on a stretcher.

Mrs. Robinson gave me a look of disgust. "This is not good," she said as we walked into the main office. "Now, we need someone to fill in for her. She's not going to be back."

"Why do you think that?" I asked.

"Mr. White, Ms. Gibbons is starting to suffer from Alzheimer's. You haven't noticed how she keeps forgetting things?"

"I hadn't really thought about it," I replied.

She is always forgetting the class schedule, I thought. *Now, I feel really bad.* I remembered that one day she asked if I would keep her keys until the end of the day and I told her no. I didn't want to do it because I felt like I didn't need any additional things to worry about.

"Ms. Deeds went to visit her at home one evening," Mrs. Robinson said. "She couldn't believe what she saw. Ms. Gibbons' apartment was extremely junky and she was practically sitting in the dark. She was just sitting in a chair with nothing on but a dim kitchen light. Mr. White, can you imagine being a highly decorated teacher for forty years and now you can't remember if you have a class coming the next period? The one consistent thing she's always had was school. Now, she's losing it. Life can be cruel sometimes," she concluded. "Now we need to figure out who is going to cover her classes. Plus, we need someone to cover Mr. Jackson's class for the next two days."

"Where is Mr. Jackson going?" I asked, pretending to be surprised.

"Ms. Deeds had to suspend him for insubordination," she replied. "He had an unexcused absence last week and didn't answer his phone when we tried to reach him. When he returned, he just said he was sick. We can't afford to have teachers miss days for no reason and not let us know."

"So who's going to take his class?"

"Ms. Deeds is going to teach while he's out."

"Have you heard anything about Mr. Howard's hiring status?" I asked.

"Nope, Ms. Deeds is supposed to meet with human resources at the end of the week and a decision will be made," Mrs. Robinson said. "Anyway, Mr. White, I have to attend a meeting with the bus company. Some kids were acting up on the bus and I need to review the tape. See you tomorrow," she said, grabbing her handbag from the desk drawer and leaving the office without another word.

What a day, I thought. *I can't wait to tell my wife about this one.*

Friday couldn't come soon enough for me. I was really looking forward to the holidays. One of the perks of being in the education field is the long holidays, especially Christmas. As I was waiting for the clock to strike 5:00pm, my phone rang. It was Mr. Howard.

"Hello, boss," he said.

"Hey, how are you, Mr. Howard?" I asked.

"Not too good. I have been trying to reach Ms. Deeds, but she won't answer my calls. Have you heard anything?"

"No, I haven't." I tried as best I could to keep my voice in neutral. In any case, I couldn't foretell what the answer would be – it could have gone either way at that juncture.

"Mr. White, I am hurting," he said. "I need a job. I have no money coming in and my rent is past due. I barely have any money to buy food. If I had known this was going to happen I would never have quit my job. I even tried to go back but they've already filled my position."

The embarrassment in his voice was audible and even painful. Even though I didn't agree with how he behaved during the retreat, I didn't think he deserved this.

"What are your plans for tonight?" I asked.

"Man, I don't have any money to do anything."

"Let me take you out to dinner," I said. "I will pick you up in an hour."

"That's cool," he replied, sounding relieved more than anything else.

Later that evening I took him to a local restaurant.

"I really appreciate you for doing this, Mr. White."

"No problem. I don't envy your predicament."

"You know, I haven't received a paycheck in almost two months. My roommate is about to put me out and I don't have anywhere to go."

With each word he pronounced, I could hear that shameful awkwardness brimming his lips. He was trying really hard to keep from crying. We sat in the restaurant for almost two hours just talking about life and how everything happens for a reason.

"Well, Mr. Howard, I need to take you home before my wife gets worried. I know it's not much, but put this in your pocket," I said while sliding him sixty dollars.

"I really do appreciate it, Mr. White," he said with a confounded smile.

He was putting the money in his wallet when my phone rang. It was Ms. Deeds.

Without much preamble, she said, "Mr. White, I need you to call Mr. Howard and tell him to report to work on Monday. He has been cleared for employment."

"Well, he is sitting across from me right now," I replied. "Do you want to tell him?"

"No, I will let you do the honors."

"Okay, I'll let him know, thanks," I said, snapping my phone shut. With a telling grin on my face I fixed my gaze on him. "Well, Mr. Howard, guess who that was?"

"I don't know, who?" he asked.

"That was Ms. Deeds. She said you have been cleared and to report to work bright and early Monday morning."

"What! What!" he screamed. "You're lying!"

The entire restaurant was now looking at us. They didn't know what was going on. Mr. Howard then literally jumped up from the table and ran outside. I could hear him yell from inside the restaurant. Everyone had turned their gazes upon him.

"He just received some really good news," I reassured everyone as I walked outside. "Mr. Howard, we need to leave before we get arrested for disturbing the peace."

"I can't believe this, Mr. White. God is good! I was really starting to question why I was going through this. Thank you, God! Thank you, Jesus!"

He was ecstatic the entire drive home. And I was extremely happy for him.

"Mr. White, I need a favor," he said. "I feel bad having to ask this, but can you loan me some money? I really need to give my roommate some money before he puts me out. I promise I will pay you back."

"How much do you need?" I turned briefly to look at his face.

"Four hundred dollars, but I will take whatever you give me," he replied.

I just gave him sixty, I thought, a little dismayed at his forwardness. *Well, I do know where he works now.*

"I will loan you the money," I agreed, "but I want you to pay me a hundred dollars every paycheck until you're paid up."

"That's fine," he said. "Trust me; I will not let you down, boss. I can't believe this," he said with joy. "God is good."

The next few weeks passed without too much trouble – if that could ever describe the upheaval that burdened our school every day – and I was starting to feel very exhausted. The long hours were beginning to really wear me down. Every day I would leave my home at 5:30am and return no earlier than 7:30pm. I was really missing my family. I was only spending about an hour a day with my wife and daughter because they were usually getting ready for bed when I returned home. I couldn't wait for the Christmas holiday.

"Ooh, Mr. White, Mr. White," Mrs. Robinson said as she came rushing into the office. "You are not going to believe this."

"Believe what?" I asked.

"It seems that a 7th grader has been spreading rumors about one of our parents having an affair with another parent."

"What!"

"I will tell you all about it later. Ms. Deeds and I have a meeting with one of the kid's parents in the next hour."

"Okay," I said, "call me after basketball practice this evening."

"Oh, I sure will. You are not going to believe this one…." She was giggling all the way down the corridor.

I had a few hours before practice so I decided to tackle the budget for next year. I had to make sure we didn't have the same hiccups as the previous two years. There were a few things I noticed immediately. The teachers were ridiculously underpaid. If you take each person's salary and divide it by the number of hours they actually worked, we were only being paid about 13 bucks an hour. That's not even counting working weekends and work done at home. It just amazed me how a job of such importance had such a low salary and was rewarded with practically no respect for what we were trying to achieve.

I guess before starting on next year's budget I should review last year's. The thing that jumped out at me immediately was the teacher roster. For some reason, all the teachers were not listed. This was a huge problem because it gave the appearance that we had more money to spend in other areas than was actually available. After going through the teacher roster, I discovered the salary of one of the English teachers was not included in the budget. That salary was obviously the reason we lost 50k the previous year. I also noticed the amount of money we received for enrollment. We received approximately 6k for each child enrolled in our school. We also received additional money for each child that had a label. So if a child was labeled as having a learning disorder, we received extra money to provide services. Basically the more labels a child had, the more money we received. We received extra money for children labeled as "at risk". *At risk* meant that they previously repeated an entire school year or had not passed the state minimum requirements test. This was the business part of the educational system that no one really discussed. I also noticed money being allocated for unnecessary things. *Why were we spending 20k on office furniture every year? Did we really need to purchase 30k worth of computer equipment every year?* This didn't sound right to me. *Why is so much money allocated towards teacher travel? Why is there so much money being spent on food for special events? What is included in "special events"?* I did see a great deal of money budgeted for school books. However, we only had a few textbooks. I was told early on that we didn't want the teachers to rely on the books to teach the kids. After reviewing the previous year's budget I became a little rattled. We had a budget of 2.2 million dollars to employ approximately 30 people and service 330 students. Therefore, the idea that the schools didn't have the money to spend was not exactly true. In fact, I could see expenditures that we needed to reduce so that we could provide more resources to the teachers. I couldn't believe we have to fight over one projector when each teacher should have one of their own. We didn't even have internet access in all the classrooms. *This doesn't make sense to me. I think next year's budget will look a lot different from the previous years. At the very least all the teachers will be listed.* I looked at my watch; *Oh well, it's time for basketball practice.*

Christmas is almost here is what I kept telling myself. As usual, I endured another morning in the cafeteria watching the kids pretending to do their morning work. *They just don't get it,* I said to myself. *They are going to regret this when they become adults.* The kids who were trying can't concentrate because the child next to them wouldn't allow it.

"How are you today, Mr. White?" said Jason.

"I am fine," I replied, "how about you?"

"You don't look fine," he said. He could clearly see that I was a little stressed.

"Let me ask you a question. Where do you see yourself in ten years?"

Jason looked confused by the question.

"What kind of question is that, Mr. White? In ten years, I will be 23 years old. I plan to be balling out of control."

"And how are you going to do that?"

"I don't know. I guess I will have a good job after I graduate from college."

"What school do you want to go to?" I asked him.

100

"I don't know yet. What school did you go to?"

"I went to Texas A&M, but I graduated from the University of Houston."

"In other words, you flunked out of A&M and you had to come back home."

"Actually, I didn't flunk out of A&M," I replied with a smile on my face.

"So why did you leave?" Clearly he didn't believe that I was telling the truth.

"I left for several reasons, but mostly because I just didn't like it."

"You didn't like it. Why did you go there if you didn't like it? I thought college was supposed to be fun."

"My parents kind of made me go. A&M offered me a scholarship, so my mother said 'that's where you are going'."

"What school did you want to go to?" he asked.

"Well, I really wanted to attend MIT."

"M – I – T, is that like ITT Tech or Devry? You know those schools that you see on the commercials," he said innocently.

"Not exactly," I chuckled. "MIT stands for Massachusetts Institute of Technology. It is the premiere school for engineering."

"So why didn't you go there? I guess you weren't smart enough?"

"Actually, Jason, I was smart enough. I just didn't have the money to pay for the application. The application fee was fifty dollars and I didn't have it."

"What?" he said in disbelief. "You didn't have fifty dollars. You couldn't ask your momma for the money? My Jordan's cost three times that much. Mr. White, ain't no way I'm going to miss college because of fifty dollars." He chuckled, getting up from his seat. "I got to go to class,

Mr. White. Let me know the next time you need fifty dollars and I will loan it to you with interest."

I had not thought about it like that before. I really wanted to go to MIT. I had gone through the interviewing process and received a letter of recommendation from one of their alumni. They all thought I was a good candidate. They even told me how to apply for financial aid. All I had to do was complete the application. However, when I finished filling it out I came across the mailing instructions. It said to mail it back along with the fifty dollar application fee. I didn't have the money. I also knew not to ask my parents for the money. So here I was, almost twenty years later, realizing that I made a fifty dollar decision that possibly changed the course of my life. What a way to start your day!

"Good morning, Mr. White," Mrs. Robinson said as she came into the office.

"Hey Mrs. Robinson," I replied. "How did the parent meeting go?"

"Oooooooh, you are not going to believe this," she said emphatically. "John Slater's parents met with Ms. Deeds and me. Mrs. Slater was upset because Aaron was telling the other kids that Mrs. Slater was having an affair with Phillip Roman's father."

"What?"

"Wait, Mr. White, that's not even the good part. Mrs. Slater went on and on about how this was hurting her son and he should not have to endure the constant teasing by the other kids. She said she wanted Aaron suspended or expelled from school. So then, Ms. Deeds said that she didn't understand why Aaron was spreading the rumors. Mrs. Slater then said, 'because it's true.' Did you hear what I said, Mr. White? She said it was true."

"You're right, Mrs. Robinson – I don't believe a word of this story! And what was Mr. Slater doing when she said that?"

"He didn't say one word. He just sat there looking like a beaten man. I couldn't believe it, Mr. White. So Ms. Deeds just looked on in amazement. The room was so quiet you could hear a rat fart," she said jokingly. "Mrs. Slater then said, what adults do in their private lives should not be discussed amongst children. She said she wanted to see something done or she was going to seek legal action."

"Legal action?" I exclaimed, "What can she do if it's true?"

"Not a damn thing, Mr. White. She's just blowing smoke. The crazy thing is that Mr. Roman is a very good looking man. He looks kind of like you. And you have seen her. She looks a mess. I don't understand why he would mess over his wife for her. You just never know why people do the things they do."

"You got that right," I said. "I can't believe that Mr. Slater just sat there."

She rose to her feet. "By the way, Mr. Goodman is on his way to drop off some more candy money," Mrs. Robinson said, apparently getting ready to leave the office once again. "Let him know that the PTA is no longer allowed to accept money from the students. From this point forward, all money must be returned to the office."

"Why the change?" I asked.

"It seems that Mr. Goodman has been complaining to Mr. Banker about money coming up short. He thinks we are stealing money. I have a meeting to attend. See you later," she added, walking out. *How demeaning it must have been for Mr. Slater,* I thought. *He must have been crushed.*

Just like clockwork, Mr. Goodman arrived right after she disappeared.

"Hello, Mr. White," he announced cheerfully as he passed the threshold of the office.

"How are you, Mr. Goodman? I heard you have some more money for me," I replied neutrally, looking up from what I was doing.

"I sure do," he said. "Now, I need you to deposit this as soon as possible."

"I will, as soon as I have an opportunity, Mr. Goodman." I smiled.

"Where's that pretty, young Mrs. Gillis?"

"She's probably teaching class," I said.

"I think I am going to drop by and say hello. I think my son is in her class right now anyway."

"Oh, before you go, Mr. Goodman," I said, "I was told to let you know that from this point on you are not to accept any more candy money. All money should be returned directly to the office."

"Who made that decision?" A look of concern draped over his face.

"We just think it's better for the children to bring the money directly to us to eliminate confusion," I said, knowing that Mr. Goodman would see right through me.

"Wait a minute, Mr. White. There wasn't any confusion. However, you are going to cause confusion now." His voice rose a decibel or two. "We were only taking the money because we were trying to give you some relief. You barely have time to make the deposits. So how are you going to be able to count the money as it comes in?"

Mr. Goodman was clearly upset. He had a point. I didn't want the responsibility, but apparently Ms. Deeds and Mrs. Robinson didn't want him to continue handling the money.

"Well, Mr. Goodman," I went on, "the fundraiser is coming to an end anyway. So I don't think there will be that much money coming in. I can handle it from here." I was trying to assure him that this wasn't a big deal.

He gave me a cold, hard stare. "Mr. White, I really don't like this and I think I need to give Ms. Deeds a call," he mumbled. "I would hate to think some funny business is going on." And with those words, he left the office with a meaningful shrug of his shoulders.

I felt stupid. I had nothing to do with this and now I had been thrown into the middle of this mess. *I don't even know who still owes us money. Once again I have to take the blame for something I had nothing to do with.*

It was the last day before the Christmas break and five o'clock could not come fast enough. Almost half the school was absent for various reasons. Some parents started early vacations. Some parents were afraid for their children to attend the last day. And some simply didn't think it was necessary for their kids to attend. Whatever the reasons, I really didn't care. I was exhausted. The long hours and stress was starting to take its toll. I needed the break more than the kids. I hadn't been this mentally drained in a long time. I always said my hardest jobs were my least paying jobs. And my easiest jobs were the highest paying. This was no exception.

"Hey, Mr. White," Mrs. Robinson said as she returned to the office.

"What's up, Mrs. Robinson?"

"You ready for the break?"

"Yes, ma'am," I replied readily enough. "I have been watching the clock for the past few hours. How about you?"

"I can't wait. Ms. Deeds, Mrs. Gillis and I are going clubbing tonight! Do you want to come?"

"Oh no – not me. I am going home and I don't plan to see or hear anything about this school until I return from the break."

"Come on, Mr. White," she urged. "Live a little. We will buy the drinks. Besides, I want to see if you can dance. You look a little stiff to me."

"Now that's a sight you will never see. I don't have time to hang out with y'all. The only person who gets to see me move is my wife. Besides, you need to be at home with your husband."

"I'm not worried about Coach," she said as Coach Robinson and Mrs. Gillis walked in.

"You're not worried about who?" he asked, grinning.

"I said that I'm worried about Coach," Mrs. Robinson repeated, looking somewhat shocked to see her husband standing in the doorway. "I am worried that you are working too hard and I don't like to see you all stressed and tired."

"Sure that's what you said," Coach Robinson said, the grin not abandoning his lips. "What's up, White? Have you all heard about Angela Turner, the sixth grader?"

"No, what happened?" Mrs. Robinson and I asked in unison.

"Ms. Deeds just told me that she won't be returning after the vacation because she is pregnant."

"WHAT!" Mrs. Robinson said emphatically. "I can't believe this. How far along is she?"

"Ms. Deeds said she was seven months," he replied.

Seven months, I thought. Angela could hide the pregnancy because she was a pretty big girl. "She may not have even known she was pregnant for some time," I said.

"Please, Mr. White, she knew," Mrs. Robinson countered. "She was probably too scared to say anything. Oh well, babies having babies. Angela has already been retained twice. More than likely she won't finish school. These kids are just ruining their lives. Well, Mr. White, I need to leave, so if I don't see you; have a great vacation," she declared amicably as she and her husband left the office.

"Same to you," I responded.

Man, I couldn't imagine having a child at thirteen, I thought. What was I doing at that age? Then it hit me like a ton of bricks. *I was having sex. At thirteen, I was three years removed from my first sexual experience.* I never realized how young I actually was. But now that I see ten-year-old students walking around campus every day, I realize that I was just a baby. *Damn, is this what I have to look forward to for my daughter when she gets this age?*

I was so engrossed in my thoughts that I didn't notice a parent had entered the office.

"Mr. White, Mr. White, are you listening?" she said.

"Oh, yes, yes, I'm here," I replied. "How are you, Ms. Morris? I haven't seen you in a while."

"Not too good. I may have to withdraw Douglas."

"Why?" I asked with great concern.

"My car isn't working and we don't have any buses close enough for him to ride to school every morning," she explained.

Ms. Morris was a really good parent. I could tell she wanted the best for her children, but I really didn't think the car was the issue.

"What can I do to help you? Where do you live?"

"We live in an apartment close to the football stadium," she replied.

"Listen, I can pick Douglas up in the mornings on my way in."

"No, Mr. White, I can't let you do that. That's too much."

"Mrs. Morris, I will be hurt if you don't let me at least try. I really like Douglas. Let me pick him up for a little while and if you don't think it's working then you can withdraw him."

"That's okay, Mr. White. Besides the transportation, I can't afford to pay the school fees. I lost my job and I'm trying to go to school. It's just not a good time for us."

"Don't worry about the fees. I'll pay them for you. What other excuse do you have?"

"Mr. White, I can't let you do all of that," she said with a tear in her eye.

I could see she was in a lot of pain. She just needed to catch a break.

"Listen, doesn't Douglas catch the bus to his grandmother's in the afternoons anyway?"

"Yes," she replied, wiping the tears from her eyes with a trembling hand.

"So picking him up in the morning is not a problem for me. Besides, he can help me open the building and setup the tables for breakfast. Trust me it's not a problem. What type of school are you attending?"

"Beauty school," she could barely say without crying.

"Good. So when you graduate, you can pay me back with a good weave job. My hairline keeps retreating from the front of my face and these crazy kids are speeding its retreat."

She couldn't help but laugh. "Okay, Mr. White. We can try it out, but I am going to pay you back."

"Don't worry about it. Douglas will pay us all back when he becomes a lawyer or a doctor."

I could tell as she walked out of the office that she was carrying a heavy burden. There was a lot more going on that she didn't want to discuss.

Five o'clock had finally arrived and I was doing my usual after school duties of walking the kids to the cars of their waiting parents. You could see my joy from a mile away.

"Hey, Mr. White," one parent yelled from her car.

"Merry Christmas, Mrs. Joy," I replied.

"I have finally figured out who you look like," she said.

"Who? Boris Kodjoe, Shemar Moore. You know the ladies love me."

"Neither one of them. You look like Madea."

"Who?"

"You know, Madea. You look like Tyler Perry."

"TYLER PERRY?" I said. "Take your child and get out of here! I don't look like him."

"Yes, you do," she said laughing. "You smile just like him."

"You know what; you can call me Tyler Perry, if you can give me some of his money."

"I know that's right," she said, driving away with a broad smile on her face.

Tyler Perry, I thought. *That's a new one. All the kids are gone and it's time for me to get out of here. Oh no, I forgot that I need to deposit that candy money. Now, how can I sneak ten thousand dollars in coins out of the building without being noticed?*

Mr. Anderson and Mrs. Robinson were in the hallway talking when I entered the building.

"What are you two doing still here?" I asked.

"We should be asking you the same question," Mrs. Robinson said with a big smile.

"Well, I'm getting out of here before some parent tries to have a conference," Mr. Anderson said as he hurried out of the building.

"See ya next week," Mrs. Robinson said to Mr. Anderson.

"Next week?" I asked. "What's happening next week?"

"Oh, nothing much. Mr. Anderson invited my family over for Christmas."

"Man, you and Mr. Anderson sure are close," I remarked.

"What's wrong with that, Mr. White?" she asked. "We are all family around here. You're the one who refuses to mingle with us outside of work."

"Listen, I don't mix family life with my work life. I don't take work home with me." *That's a big lie,* I thought. *All I talk about at home is work and all the craziness that goes on here.* "Mrs. Robinson, can I ask you a question?"

"Sure, what's up?"

"When are you going to admit that you and Mr. Anderson are related?"

The silence was deafening. I could see her face flush. She immediately pushed me into the office and closed the door.

"Mr. White…, Mr. White, you cannot tell a soul," she begged. I could hear the desperation in her voice.

"I won't say anything," I assured her.

"How did you know?"

"Well, when you told me 'we attended the same high school', I decided to do a little research. I looked in the school year book and found your picture. Of course you went by your maiden name back then which happened to be Anderson. So how are you related?"

"Mr. White, you cannot tell a soul," she pleaded again. "Mr. Anderson is my brother."

I wasn't expecting to hear that, I thought.

"Your secret is safe with me," I assured her.

She was still clearly rattled. She quickly gathered her things, wished me a happy holiday and left the building. I wasn't going to tell anyone. I really liked Mrs. Robinson and Mr. Anderson. Besides, they both represented what was good about the school. The kids need both of them here. I did think it was hypocritical of Mrs. Robinson though, because she hated the fact that Ms. Ebony and Ms. Lloyd worked here and were sisters. She thought they used that to gang up on Ms. Deeds. But Mrs. Robinson had them beat. Her husband and brother both worked here. *Oh well, I need to get this money into the car and get out of here. I have to get over to Davenport's to meet up with two of my old friends.*

Interlude - Believing

This is the basketball story. I separated this from the rest of the book because I thought the story had a life of its own. The highs and lows of the season should really be told in an additional book which I may embark on in the future. Instead I want to share one of the most important moments of the season that I feel is a universal story to which anyone can relate.

All season I had been trying to instill the idea of believing in my boys. I never envisioned the idea would grow to the level it had. The boys had grown to believe in not only themselves but they believed and trusted each other. We went from a losing record of 1 win and 5 losses to finishing the regular season with 18 wins and 6 losses.

Post season play had begun and we were favored to reach the finals. We steamrolled through the first two rounds and I could sense my boys were a little overconfident, which scared me. We were about to be tested in the semifinal round however. We had to play the team who was favored to win the tournament – Power Prep. We played them earlier in the season and we lost to them by five points. I racked my brain the night before, thinking about how we could beat this team.

Then I recalled when I first realized how powerful the brain could be. I was in college and was working on a project that was extremely difficult. I could not figure out how to solve this one equation and had fallen asleep thinking of ways to find the answer. Remarkably, the solution came to me in the form of a dream. The next morning I was able to complete the project and I had a new-found respect for the power of the brain. So I decided that I was going to dream about the game the night before. I lay in bed and all I thought about was the game and how we could win. Eventually, I fell asleep and just as in college I found the answer to my problem.

The next day I picked up the boys in the school van and we made our way to the tournament. I could sense that the kids were not ready. When we walked into the gym the crowd was hyped up. Power Prep had a really strong following just like we had. Their fans and our fans practically filled the entire gym. The other schools that played earlier were also in attendance. Before I knew it, the game had begun. The pace of the game started off fast. They would score and we would score. It was back and forth. However, they kept scoring and we were starting to miss. It wasn't long before they were leading by 10 points and my boys were looking a little worried. Then we were down by 20 points and now I was looking worried. This was not how I envisioned it. This did not happen in my dream. We went into halftime trailing by 20 points, but I reassured my boys that we had an answer. We came out in the second half with more energy and managed to decrease their lead to 10 points. Unfortunately, they were well coached and their kids were very good athletes. They were disciplined and it didn't take long before they figured out what we were doing. Before long, they increased their lead back up to 20 points and my boys were again discouraged. All the while I kept thinking this is not a part of my dream. We won in my dream.

We lost the game by 30 points. My boys were very emotional in the locker room afterwards; they thought our entire season was a failure because we lost. I then explained to them our season was not over.

"This is a double elimination tournament," I explained. "It means that we could lose one game and still have a shot at the finals."

They looked at me blankly and didn't understand what I said. I explained a loss just meant we had to play an additional game against the team coming out of the loser's bracket.

"Listen," I said. "We beat the team coming out of the loser's bracket early in the tournament. We are going to beat them again and then we will play Power Prep one last time. However, this time we are going to kick their ass and we are going to be champions!"

The boys couldn't believe it. I knew the language was strong but I needed to give them the confidence they needed.

We easily won our next game, setting up the showdown with Prep. We were sitting in the locker room getting ready for our final game. The tension was palpable. We could hear the gym starting to fill to capacity as the anticipation of what was about to happen swelled.

"Are you ready?" I asked.

"Yes, Sir!" they hollered in unison.

"All season I've told you about the power of believing and you bought in. I am proud of you all for believing in yourselves, believing in each other and believing in me. If you believe, you can make your wildest dreams come true."

The boys were listening attentively and studying my every word.

"I believe," I said. "I believe we will win tonight. I know we are going to win, because I dreamed it."

I could see the puzzled looks all around the room.

"We are going to win!" I exclaimed. "And this is how we are going to do it. Who here has heard of the 1-3-1 zone?"

Only two or three boys knew what I was referring to. Because of our short practice time, I wasn't able to teach them many offensive or defensive plays, so we only played man-to-man defense. I decided to give them a quick demonstration and trimmed down version of the defense. I showed each of them the spots they would occupy.

"As long as you keep your positions we will be fine." I could sense their confusion. "Just believe and listen to me and you will be fine," I reassured them.

We came out of the locker room to a gym that was standing room only. There was a tremendous buzz in the air. I could taste victory and the game had not even started. Power Prep was already on the court taking warm up shots. They were the definition of confidence.

"Listen," I said to my boys, "we have 15 minutes before tip-off. I want you to sit on the bench and think about what we are about to do. Oh, by the way," I added, "I want all of you to do what I do when I tell you."

They did as I told them, but looked even more puzzled, wondering what I wanted them to do.

We watched Prep as they horsed around on the court. They knew they were going to beat us a third time and be crowned champions.

The clock was now at 10 minutes.

I could see our fans starting to settle into their seats and looking in our direction. The other teams were choosing sides and making predictions.

The clock now read 5 minutes.

I started to replay the season in my mind. I never imagined being in this position. I had fallen out of love with this sport, which, I felt didn't love me. And here I was passionately wanting my lost love to love my boys. *Give them the experience I never was able to get from this cruel love of mine.*

The clock read 2 minutes.

My heart was pounding. I began to pace the sidelines furiously. *This is it,* I thought. I closed my eyes and took a deep breath. At that moment I could hear only my voice.

"We ready, we ready," I began to sing. This was a sports' chant we used to sing when I played basketball. It had the tone of an old Negro spiritual.

"We ready for y'all," I sang while pacing the sidelines. No one could really hear me because the gym was so loud. However, they could see me.

"We ready, we ready, we ready for y'all," I began shouting as I pumped my fist to the rhythm of the chant.

People were beginning to take notice of what I was doing. My boys were looking at me with confusion and embarrassment. Some people were laughing and pointing in my direction.

"We ready, we ready, we ready for y'all," I shouted with renewed vigor.

By this time Prep began to warm up and was starting to count their repetitions loudly so as to drown me out.

"1 one thousand, 2 one thousand," they repeated in unison.

"Sing with me," I said to my boys. "We ready, we ready, we ready for y'all."

At first they were reluctant to follow in singing. However, our fans began to take notice as did Prep's fans.

"3 one thousand, 4 one thousand," Prep began shouting louder.

"Stand up," I told my boys. "Stand up and sing louder!"

"We ready, we ready, we ready for y'all!" we began to yell while directing our fire towards the opposing team.

Remarkably our fans started to chant with us. Prep's fans began chanting with their team. Before long the entire gym was chanting with the team they were supporting.

"We ready, we ready, we ready for y'all," we sang.

"1 one thousand, 2 one thousand," they chanted loudly.

It sounded like two massive choirs battling for supremacy. It was unbelievable. I was yelling at the top of my lungs. My boys were jumping up-and-down. The adrenaline was through the roof. The gym was an absolute, organized chaos. The other coaches were smiling from ear to ear.

The clock expired and the buzzer sounded for the game to begin.

I leaned over and whispered to one of the officials. "Do you think they are ready?"

He looked at me in amazement. "I think they are ready, Coach," he replied.

The game started like our last match. It was fast paced and both teams were going back and forth. They would score a basket and we would score. Both teams increased their defensive intensity. They would stop us from scoring then we would not let them score. However, they began slowly to take control of the game. Just like the last game, they began to build a lead. They would score and we would not. I could feel the momentum beginning to build in their favor. Our fans' cheers had lost steam. There was a sense of "here we go again" starting to build as they built their lead up to 10 points.

"Timeout," I yelled to the referee as the clock read 7 minutes until half time.

I looked at my boys and they looked at me. They were attentively waiting for me to give them an answer to this Prep puzzle.

"Now is the time," I said confidently. "Run the defense like I showed you and watch what happens."

I could not have written a better script. We came out of the time out and set up in the defense. The first play Prep attempted to run we got a steal and scored. The next play, we blocked their shot attempt and scored again. The crowd was back in our corner. The energy level began to rise again. Before I knew it the game was tied. It became a defensive seesaw match with no one being able to score. However, we started to find ways to make baskets while they couldn't. Then their coaches started to get frustrated as we increased our lead by 10 points.

The gym was overflowing with excitement. With only one minute before halftime we were performing extremely well. However, Prep was a really good team and they were able to cut our lead down to five before the buzzer sounded.

I sensed my boys felt they could really win this game as we headed to the locker room. Prep looked discouraged and dejected.

Before we entered our side of the locker room, we could see the Prep coaches chastising their players in the hallway.

"Stop," I told my boys. "Look at them." I felt like Muhammad Ali when he fought Sonny Liston. "Look at them," I shouted. "They're scared. They don't want to come back and play us. They don't want to play us anymore." I pointed in their direction. "They know we're better than them."

I yelled just loud enough for my boys to hear, but just soft enough that Prep's coaches did not hear me. I did not want to give them bulletin board material; however, I wanted my boys to feel like they were the best team.

"Listen," I said calmly as we entered the locker room, "we still have one half left. We must complete the mission. We are going to win this game. I've already dreamed this."

As I expected Prep made adjustments after halftime and erased our lead. But this time, my boys were not discouraged. The game continued to seesaw back and forth. They would score and we would score. I needed something different. I needed a spark to get us back into the lead. I found that spark as we began the fourth quarter in the form of my smallest, most unreliable player. His name was Adrian. I couldn't play Adrian very often because he was too wild. He was a great football player, but basketball wasn't really his sport. My wife thought he was the cutest little thing on the team. Adrian had a gift and that was the gift of speed. He was as quick as lightning.

"Adrian, you're coming in," I said as if this was normal.

He wasn't used to me playing him much, especially in a crucial game, so he was slow to rise.

"Adrian, hurry up," I said.

He took off his jacket and ran to me.

"You know how I always fuss at you for playing too wild?" I asked. "Well I want you to be you."

"What?" he blurted in total disbelief. "What do you mean?"

"I want you to play all out. Don't worry about me getting mad at you. I don't want you to slow down for anyone. Wherever the ball goes that's where you go."

Adrian was shocked, but seemed relieved that I was going to let him play his out of control style of basketball. Right before he entered the game I grabbed him by the arm.

"Look at me," I said. "I don't care who has the ball. You take it and you score. Don't worry about committing fouls. Don't worry about missing shots."

"Okay, Coach," he said with a grin.

Adrian entered the game and I could see he still didn't believe me. For the first time, he was playing under control which was not what I needed him to do.

"Adrian," I screamed. "Go get the ball! Take the ball from him."

He acted as if he didn't understand. Then the boys sitting on the bench started to yell for him to take the ball as well.

Then it was like his light switch turned on. Adrian must've run what seemed like 100 mph and stole the ball from the Prep player. He made a straight line to the basket and did something he was never able to do. He made a lay-up. The crowd went crazy. The very next play, he did the exact same thing again. He stole the ball, ran to the other end of the court and scored. The people in the stands were in an uproar. Unbelievably, he stole the ball a third time. This time a defender decided to foul him as he attempted to make the lay-up.

Unfortunately, Adrian was not a good free-throw shooter. Sometimes when he shot, the ball did not even make it to the rim.

"Make sure you get the rebound," I shouted to the boys.

However, Adrian had other plans. He nailed the first free-throw and the crowd went absolutely berserk. Remarkably, he nailed the second free throw while the spectators went totally crazy. We were then ahead by eight points and Prep was looking stunned. The game continued to sway back and forth, but we continued to lead by eight.

My spark plug, Adrian, was showing signs of fatigue and was committing too many fouls. Prep started to make another run and cut the lead down to four points with only two minutes left in the game. My star center was extremely exhausted because he had played almost the entire game, so I had to give him a break. The only back up I had available was Stanley. Stanley was not blessed with quick feet and couldn't jump any higher than an inch. However, he could fill space.

"Stanley," I called.

He ran to me clearly afraid. "Yes, Coach," he said.

"Do you remember why you said you wanted to play basketball?" I asked.

"Yes, sir," he replied, "because I wanted to lose weight."

"Well, Stanley, I kept my end of the bargain and you were able to lose a few pounds. And now I need you to help me."

"What do you need me to do?"

"Akeem needs some rest. I need you to play for one minute and I want you to play the best one minute you have ever played in your life. Can you do that, Stanley?"

"I can do it, Coach," he said confidently.

I looked at Stanley's eyes and I believed him. He ran out onto the court and I could hear snickering from the stands. Stanley was a very big kid and his uniform was extremely tight on him, which provoked some amused comments among the people sitting on the bleachers.

However, Stanley did not listen and did exactly what I wanted him to do. In his first play on defense, a little boy tried to drive into the lane and Stanley stood his ground. It looked as though the boy ran into a brick wall. They charged Stanley with a foul but the message was clear. If you come into the lane, he will send you packing.

We now had the ball on offense and we were having a difficult time scoring. My best shooter Ricky missed a long shot; however, Stanley was able to get the rebound even though he only jumped about a centimeter off the ground. Although Stanley rarely shot the ball, he had made up his mind that he was going to have the game of his life. He shot the ball back up and scored. We were all shocked.

The crowd was hysterical. Stanley pumped his fist in the air as he ran back down to the other end.

Now with only 30 seconds left in the game we were up by two points and Prep called a timeout.

"Hurry, guys," I yelled to my team. "Here's what we need to do."

They could almost taste victory and their emotions were starting to consume them.

Then Charles said, "Coach, I believe."

It was like time just stopped. My heart was pounding. My eyes were about to water. I could not believe what he had just said. All year I felt I had not made a difference but at that moment I felt a tremendous sense of pride. The other boys started saying it as well. I was overcome with joy.

I looked at them as a proud father would look at his sons.

"I'm happy that you believe," I said. "But I need you to believe real hard for 30 more seconds so we can win this game."

Prep quickly came out of the time out and tried to score. However, Akeem, who had reentered the game, rejected the shot. We got the rebound, ran to the other end of the court and scored. Prep again ran down the court and tried to score quickly. This time we stole the ball, ran down to the other end of the court and scored. The clock now read 10 seconds and we were beginning to celebrate. The fans were going crazy. I was going crazy. And finally the buzzer rang and the game was over. Our fans rushed the court and I let out a loud scream.

I could not believe what just happened. This was the most unbelievable game I've ever been a part of. It was symbolic of our season. We started off extremely rough. I lost boys because of grades, discipline problems, drugs and family issues. However, this group of boys was able to accomplish something no one believed they could. We practiced in a church cafeteria and traveled in a passenger van. Over the course of one season those boys became young men. These memories will stay with them for the rest of their lives. When they become adults they will talk about this day as if it happened yesterday. I will never forget what they were able to accomplish that day and they are now permanently etched in my life and in my mind.

Out with the old

"The Davenport" is certainly aptly named. The comfortable setting is inviting for the patrons to relax and have a drink among friends. And that was exactly what I intended to do.

As I walked in I immediately heard my friend Tony's voice yell, "White, White, get on the line!"

He was imitating our old basketball coach who used to yell at us every chance he got.

"What's up, boy?" I said as we hugged.

We had not seen each other in over ten years. We had stopped being friends basically over a woman. Fortunately, we reconnected via Facebook.

"How have you been?" he asked.

"Man, I can't complain," I said. "What about you? I heard you turned into this big time basketball player overseas."

"Man, White, those days are over. Now, I'm just enjoying life."

"Well, if it isn't Batman and Robin!" someone yelled from the other side of the bar.

It was my best friend, Jacob. He was the third member of our high school crew. Jacob and I had kept in touch over the years, but he had not seen Tony in a while either.

"What's up, Mr. Smooth," Tony said as they greeted each other.

Jacob was the "cool" guy in the group. He dressed really nice and had this old school persona about him.

"What's up, White?" Jacob asked, turning his face to me.

"It sure is good to see us three together again," I replied with a broad grin. And indeed it was good to find the three of us in one place after being apart for all those years.

I could feel the brotherly love. I really missed my boys and I could tell they felt the same.

"Let's get some drinks flowing up in here," Tony said.

We talked for hours about what we had been doing for the past ten years.

"White, I heard you were a teacher now," Tony said.

"Yep, I work at a charter school," I replied, cracking a smile.

"Do you like it?" he asked.

"It's been a real eye opener. Our kids are in trouble. It's different from when we were in school. Back then you had one or two problem kids in a classroom and everyone else was somewhat normal. Now, it seems like you have one or two normal kids in a classroom and everyone else is off the chain. One thing that I've really noticed is the anger coming from the boys. Half the boys at our school have some sort of anger management label or need medication to control their temper."

"Man, White, you used to walk around pretty angry back in the day too," Tony joked. "I remember when I would pick you up from your house after something had happened and we would just ride around not saying a word."

"I had forgotten about that," I said.

"A lot of these boys are angry because they don't have any real fathers around," Tony said.

"I don't know if that's a good excuse," said Jacob. "I haven't seen my father since I was three, but I didn't act like that."

"But you at least had your uncle," Tony argued.

"Jacob, I didn't know your father wasn't around at all," I said.

"Man, my father was there, but sometimes I wished he wasn't," Tony said. "He used to come to our games drunk and the police would have to escort him out."

"What! You know I don't remember ever meeting your father," I said, somewhat shocked to learn that Tony's father was an alcoholic.

"That's because I was too ashamed to acknowledge him," Tony added ruefully.

Here we were three adult men who grew up together. We went to the same school, played basketball together and hung out all the time. But this was the first time we had ever discussed our relationships with our fathers. We sat and swapped stories that we had never revealed before. It was therapeutic, but also sad. Ideally, your friends are the ones you confide in when things aren't going well. We were really good friends who had not revealed anything of their troubles until now. We just dealt with it internally as we had been taught. *This is why I have to make a difference at this school,* I thought. *Somehow or other I have to reach these children before it's too late.*

We had one more week of vacation before we returned to school. And while I was enjoying my time with my family, when Mrs. Robinson called me to have a meeting to discuss our plans for the second semester, I jumped at the opportunity.

"Hey, Mrs. Robinson," I said as she reached the table, "how's your vacation going?"

"What vacation?" she asked. "I haven't had one day of rest since I left campus. Ms. Deeds has been chewing me out, because Banker has been tearing into her. Banker is complaining about the student enrollment, our budget and anything else he can think of."

"Okay, Mrs. Robinson, I think it's time for you to be honest with me," I said. "What is really going on with the school? Before I started working here I was really impressed with the students and staff. I thought you were the model of what a school should be. However, my feelings have changed. Ms. Deeds is never around and seems to have an excuse for everything. Ms. Ebony is the assistant principal, but I rarely see her outside of her classroom. I feel like we are running the school and that's not what I came here to do. I only wanted to teach. That's it."

"I understand how you feel, Mr. White," Mrs. Robinson said. "Believe me, I wish things were operating better. As you know, Ms. Deeds is going through a divorce, plus her mother and brother are having some health issues. So she is really having a rough time right now. You know I don't care for Ms. Ebony. She has always been a burden on Ms. Deeds. I wish Ms. Deeds would just fire her."

"What about Mr. Jackson?" I asked.

"What about him?"

"You know what I'm talking about. The rumors have been swirling around for quite some time now. Is Ms. Deeds having an affair with Mr. Jackson?"

"Not anymore," she replied. "As far as I know, they broke it off. I never trusted Mr. Jackson. He's a real snake."

"Why do you say that?" I asked.

"I can't really put my finger on it, but trust me he is. Listen, Mr. White, I am not going to sit here and lie to you. We have some issues. I have been trying to keep this ship afloat by myself, but I need help."

I could sense the desperation in her voice.

"Okay, Mrs. Robinson, you got me. You've been trying to get me to be vocal and take charge. Well, now you are going to get what you asked for."

"What does that mean, Mr. White?" she asked, taken aback by my readiness to do battle.

"It means we are going to take over this school and run it the way it's supposed to be run," I replied confidently.

We talked for several hours devising a plan on how we were going to get the school where it needed to be.

"First, we are going to start enforcing all the rules that none of the students seemed to follow," I said. "Dress code violations, tardiness, excessive absences, and disrespectful behavior will no longer be tolerated. Second, we are going to remove some of the kids that have been terrorizing the other students and teachers. Third, we are going to market the school and really recruit kids that are ready for a college prep school. Last, we are going to recruit quality teachers who share the same vision as we do. We just have to get Ms. Deeds to go along with the program."

"That won't be a problem," she said. "I will take care of her. Besides, if she's not around, we can run the school as we see fit."

It was, by all means, an ambitious plan, but one that needed to be put into motion if we cared at all for the future of not only the school as a whole, but also for the future of each child attending it.

The first day of school after the break quickly approached and Mrs. Robinson and I were ready with our guns fully loaded.

"Are you ready, Mr. White?" she asked.

"Oh, I'm ready," I replied, smiling.

We walked into the cafeteria that morning greeted by the usual loud and unruly group of students.

"Okay, listen up," Mrs. Robinson demanded. As always, she was really good at controlling a large group of people. "It has come to my attention that you have been busy doing everything, but what you are supposed to be doing in this cafeteria. From this point on I do not want to hear a single voice in this cafeteria unless it is a teacher or you are addressing a teacher! From this point on all morning work will be turned in to your first period teacher. It will be graded and you will receive a zero if you do not turn it in. Do you understand me?"

"Yes, Mrs. Robinson," the children answered in unison.

"It has also come to my attention that several of you have decided the school dress code does not apply to you," she went on. "If you come to school out of dress code, we will call your parents to pick you up or bring the appropriate clothing. Do you understand me?"

"Yes, Mrs. Robinson," the kids replied in one voice once again.

"Now having said that, if Mr. White calls your name, please gather your things and lineup at the door," she added, looking up at me.

"I need the following students," I said and then called the names of approximately fifty students.

Once they all lined up, I announced, "These students are out of dress code. Please walk down to the office and prepare to call your parents."

The entire cafeteria was quiet. The students could not believe it. I could see some of them tucking in their shirts and hiding jewelry that they were not supposed to be wearing.

We made a lot of parents upset that morning.

"Mr. White, I don't appreciate your having my child sit in the office because she is out of dress code," said the infamous Ms. Russell. "I cannot believe you are making parents leave work over a silly dress code."

"Well, Ms. Russell, we have rules that we all must abide by," I answered. "Don't you have to follow a certain dress code at your place of business, Mrs. Russell?"

"Please, don't try to compare this little school to my job. If this school doesn't get its act together I may have to withdraw my child."

I wish she would, I thought, and added, "Oh, by the way, Ms. Russell, I have not received the lunch application from you. Do you need another one?"

She gave me a really evil glare and walked out of the office with her daughter.

It really amazes me how negative some parents can be towards the people who teach their children. Most of the parents who came to the school told me they didn't realize we had a dress code. However, they understood and assured me this would not happen again. Just as the last parent departed, I heard a loud scream coming from a classroom down the hall.

"Mr. White! Mr. White! They're fighting!" someone hollered.

When I arrived in the classroom two girls were yelling and cursing at one another and Mr. Holly was picking himself off the ground.

"I need some help," he said with a worried look on his face.

Apparently the girls were fighting, but had been separated by the time I arrived. However, they were still trying to get to each other. One student, Jasmine, was being held by two boys. Mr. Holly was trying to hold Cassie back, without much success. Being free once again, she was pushing and trying to get close to Jasmine. Cassie was a big, strong girl, but I wasn't about to allow her or any other student to get the better of me physically.

"Cassie, this is me," I whispered into her ear. "You better turn around and head to the office before you have to deal with me."

She must have detected the seriousness in my voice, because she stopped immediately and went straight to the office. Once order had been restored, I returned to the office to speak to the trouble-maker. I was going to suspend both girls, but I really wanted to talk with Cassie first. Even though this was her first year in the school, she had been involved in two fights and numerous confrontations.

"Okay, what happened this time, Cassie?" I asked her.

"Ooh, Mr. White, I don't want to be here anymore," she burst out, letting tears flow down her cheeks. "I hate coming here every day! They talk about my hair, my weight! I just can't take this anymore! They always call me names. Blacky! Darkey! Slut! I hate them! Please kick me out! I don't care anymore!"

"First, I need you to calm down," I said. "We can't have a civil conversation if you are hysterical. Let me know when you are ready."

She sat there for a few minutes looking puzzled while I answered emails on my computer. I gave her some tissue to wipe her face and continued working. She was expecting me to yell at her, but I didn't. I just waited until she was ready.

"I'm ready now, Mr. White," she said when several minutes had passed and she didn't hear any reaction from me.

"Okay," I said while turning to face her. "Why are you continuing to have problems with your classmates?"

"It's not me, it's them!" she screamed in reply.

"Wait, Cassie…, you said you were ready, but you are still yelling."

"I'm sorry, Mr. White," she apologized. "People are always talking about how dark I am. It hurts my feelings."

Cassie did not fit the mold of the pretty, prissy girl which she desired to be. She had very prominent facial features. Her hair was not very long and she was overweight. To make matters worse she was going through puberty, so her body was starting to develop.

"Cassie, I could tell you that everything is going to be alright and not to worry about what people say, but I am not. The harsh reality is that you are probably going to be ridiculed and judged because of the way you look for the rest of your life. However, you can change the way people see you if you change the way you see yourself."

She looked even more puzzled and confused.

"Do you think Mrs. Robinson is pretty?" I asked.

"Mrs. Robinson is very pretty," she replied.

"Well, she is as dark as you," I noted, emphasizing the fact. "Yet, she walks around here like she's on the red carpet. She flings her hair so much my neck gets sore, and her hair is as short as yours." I looked at Mrs. Robinson who was sitting at her desk and could see she was about to burst. "Mrs. Robinson encountered the same issues when she was as young as you. However, she overcame them by loving herself. No one loves Mrs. Robinson more than Mrs. Robinson."

"That's right, Mr. White," Mrs. Robinson piped up as she left the office. "You know I'm sexy. Watch out now!"

"Look at me," I said to Cassie. "Do you know how many jokes I've heard about my big eyebrows? I know they are huge, but my wife loves them. Look at my big head. My body had to catch up to it. It took me a while to realize I needed this big head to hold all this knowledge I have."

Cassie was getting a good laugh at my expense and was starting to feel better. Unfortunately, we both knew that feeling would be short-lived if she didn't truly believe in what I said.

"Cassie, I suggest you start talking to Mrs. Robinson and just watch how she does things."

"I will, Mr. White," Cassie replied, somewhat appeased. "Thanks for the talk. I really needed that."

"No problem," I said. "However, you need to call your mother and let her know you are going to be out for a few days. I haven't forgotten about the fight."

Suddenly, Ms. Deeds walked into the office. "I heard we had some drama today," she said. "Cassie, you really want to get kicked out don't you? You keep it up and you'll get your wish."

Cassie just sat in her chair motionless – looking up at Ms. Deeds as if she was the devil personified.

"Mr. White, we need to get with Mrs. Robinson and decide how we are going to celebrate the inauguration," she went on, ignoring Cassie and the ensuing drama that her remark might have provoked. "We'll all be wearing our Sunday's finest, including Mr. Jackson."

"Wait a minute, does he even own a suit?" I asked.

Mr. Jackson was not the type to wear suits. He would walk around barefoot if he could.

"He has one now," Ms. Deeds replied. "I took him to buy one this past weekend."

I can't believe what I just heard, I thought. *I guess they are still messing around.*

"Oh yeah, Mr. White," she said as she left the office, "I am going to be out for the rest of the week." *Surprise, surprise*, I thought. "I will be moving to my new apartment and I need to make sure the movers don't destroy my things."

I guess she is really moving forward with her divorce. And I guess she doesn't care who knows since she just said that in front of everybody.

"Okay," I said, "we will hold down the fort."

It was the end of the week and the students were having a difficult time adjusting to our new found structure. We had to suspend several students for various violations including fighting, skipping class and swearing at teachers. However, I believed our plan was working. The kids were starting to straighten their lines when Mrs. Robinson or I walk down the halls.

"Good morning, Mr. White," said Jason.

"Good Morning," I replied.

"Mr. White, no disrespect, but you've changed. You used to be nice. Now, you don't play around."

"That's a good observation, Jason."

Get used to it, I thought. These kids needed structure and discipline. I liked being able to walk down the hallways and not hear anyone yell and scream. The kids responded to me differently now. I was no longer the new teacher. I had become the person to fear. The person that would call your parents or send you home in a heartbeat. *No more Mr. "Nice" White*, I thought as I patrolled the halls of the school. He died on December 31st. Mr. "Doomsday" White was now on campus and I was taking no prisoners.

"Hey, Boss," Mr. Holly said as I walked past his classroom.

"How's it going, Holly?" I asked.

"Lovely, just lovely. I really appreciate everything you've done for me. Here is the first installment of the loan you gave me." He handed me one hundred dollars.

"Thanks," I replied, pocketing the money.

"I have another favor to ask of you," he said. "Do you think there is any way I can ride with you to work? I have to catch three buses to make it here on time."

"I don't know, Mr. Holly. You really don't live close to me and I have someone else riding with me in the morning."

"No, no, no, you don't have to pick me up at my house," he said emphatically. "I would never ask you to go out of your way. However, one of the buses I catch has a stop on your route to work. You could just pick me up from there. I just need a ride until I get a few paychecks. Then I can get a car."

I paused a few seconds before answering, because I was still on the fence with him. I didn't know if he was a good hire or not.

"We can try it out," I suggested.

He smiled. "Thanks, Boss. I really appreciate it, Boss."

I didn't like the way he called me "Boss". He spoke with a heavy southern drawl. It caused me to see visions of slavery whenever he called me "Boss". I couldn't tell if he used it as a term of flattery or if he felt like he was working on the plantation.

"Hey, Mr. White," said Monique. Monique was Ms. Lilly's oldest daughter.

"Hello, Monique," I replied. "What are you doing here?"

"Mother asked me to pick up some of the boys so they could straighten the house for the boys' sleepover this weekend."

Every other month Ms. Lilly would have a sleepover for some of the kids. She was really going above and beyond the call of duty by opening her home to them. This particular weekend the 7th grade boys were staying over and Coach Robinson and Mr. Steel were chaperoning them.

"Make sure you sign them out in the office," I said to her as she headed in that direction.

"Okay, I will," she said, turning her head back to me.

A few weeks had passed and the school was really starting to take shape. The majority of the students were following the rules and I could sense the teachers were not as stressed.

"Mr. White, Mr. White, we need to talk," Mrs. Robinson said as she rushed into the office.

"What's up?" I asked.

"Mr. Banker is on the warpath," she said. "He received a call from a friend who stated she saw several students eating at a restaurant during school hours a few weeks ago."

"Okay, so what does that have to do with us?" I asked.

"They were wearing our uniforms. The descriptions she gave of the students were clearly some of our boys. Did you allow some of the boys to leave campus a few weeks ago?"

"Not exactly, Ms. Lilly's daughter picked up a few of them to help cleanup for a sleepover."

"You do know that students aren't allowed to leave campus without their parents' permission?" she asked.

I could see where this conversation was going.

"Wait one minute Mrs. Robinson. Ms. Lilly has held several sleepovers and I know Ms. Deeds allowed students on several occasions to help prepare for them during school hours. Don't try to put this on me. Besides, two of the boys that left were Ms. Lilly's sons."

"Well, Mr. Banker is on his way to the school as we speak and he is saying that someone is going to be fired," Mrs. Robinson stated. "Ms. Deeds is on her way as well."

I couldn't believe that the finger was being pointed at me. I couldn't count how many times students had left campus to do things for Ms. Deeds. I couldn't wait for Banker to get here. However, I didn't see him at all that day. Apparently, he came in through the back door, ripped into Ms. Deeds and Ms. Lilly and departed. Unfortunately, we had an emergency meeting after school to discuss what had transpired.

"Well," Ms. Deeds said to the entire staff. "I don't know if I am going to have my job after this weekend. It was brought to my attention that some students were allowed to miss class so they could clean up for some planned sleepover. Mr. Banker ordered me to fire Ms. Lilly or be fired." Everyone looked stunned. "As much as I love Ms. Lilly, she did endanger the lives of our students. God forbid had something tragic happened the school would've been liable."

I couldn't believe what I was hearing. Ms. Lilly would give her life for these kids.

"Wait, Ms. Deeds, I have to say something," said Ms. Ebony. "My son was one of the boys who left and I wasn't notified. I don't know what I would have done if something had happened to him."

I was shocked that Ms. Ebony was saying this. She personally had taken kids off campus on many occasions without their parents knowing. At least every other month, she would take the Dance team to different performances around the city. I am pretty sure most of their parents didn't know their children were missing school.

"So what are you going to do?" I asked Ms. Deeds.

"I had to let Ms. Lilly go," she replied. "She was terminated effective immediately."

There was a stunned silence in the room. *So I guess that means Ms. Deeds isn't getting fired*, I thought.

"Ms. Lilly was told to leave the campus immediately," Ms. Deeds repeated. "She will be back this evening to collect her things. Let this be a warning to everyone else. We have to tighten up. When things like this happen I am the one whose head goes on the chopping block."

Mrs. Robinson and I looked at one another as if to say, "We need to talk." I tried to wait around campus after the meeting for Ms. Lilly to return, but I also had to take Mr. Holly home. I wanted to know what happened in her meeting with Banker. *Hopefully our paths will cross sooner rather than later,* I thought.

The next few days were very somber. The students heard the bad news and the entire sixth grade class was basically in mourning.

"Good morning, Mr. White," Mrs. Robinson said as she walked into the office.

"Good morning," I replied flatly.

"I don't know if Ms. Deeds told you, but we have to change the 6th grade team's schedule to accommodate the loss of Ms. Lilly," Mrs. Robinson went on. "Mrs. Hollins is going to teach Math now."

"How is she going to teach Math and Social Justice?" I asked.

"She's not. We are going to remove Social Justice from the schedule and extend the other classes by 20 minutes."

"Mrs. Robinson, it seems like we are changing the students' schedules every month. This is not good for them. For most of these kids, we are probably their only source of stability." Mrs. Robinson nodded. "We cannot do this to these children and expect them to just roll with the punches. How do you think these kids feel? They come to school every morning not knowing what to expect, because every day we change something. We have teachers dropping like flies. We change their schedules every five minutes. We cancel electives because our principal doesn't like who's teaching them. We cancel gym because certain students are not acting properly. One week lunch is in the cafeteria, the next week they have to eat in their classrooms. I don't blame the kids for being disobedient. Hell, this is driving me crazy."

"Mr. White, I agree with everything you've said," Mrs. Robinson said. "However, I am not the school leader, so there is only so much I can do. If this were my school, things would be different."

"We are practically running the school now," I countered. "Ms. Deeds is never here. We are the ones that take the heat for all this foolishness. I don't understand how she keeps her job. How hard can it be to start your own school? We need to do something, because this is not working."

"Actually, it's not that difficult at all," she said. "Mr. White, we have the blueprint right here. All we need is a charter from the state."

"It sounds like you have researched this already," I said.

"I have. My dream is to lead my own school."

"Well, hell, let's do it then," I said.

"Let's do what?" she asked, visibly puzzled.

"Let's start our own school! We can't possibly be as bad as this one."

"Mr. White, you can't just start a state-funded charter school," Mrs. Robinson said. "The application process takes more than a year."

"That gives us just enough time to do all the research and get this thing going."

"Are you serious? Don't play with me."

"I am very serious."

"Mr. White, this is my dream. I don't want you to get me all excited and then you flake out on me."

"Don't worry, Mrs. Robinson. We have to do something to correct the damage this school has done. I'm all in."

"Okay, let's plan to meet on the weekends to discuss how we are going to accomplish this. I don't want anyone to catch wind of this."

"My lips are sealed," I assured her.

I could sense a renewed energy in Mrs. Robinson as she left the office. I felt reenergized myself. *This was my chance to really make a change,* I thought.

"Hello, Mr. White, how are you today?" I heard someone say. It was Roy Jackson's mother along with his grandmother.

"Hey, Jackson family, I'm great. How are you all doing today?" I asked.

"Not too good," Roy's mother replied. "We are here to see Ms. Deeds regarding Roy's grades and conduct."

"Was she expecting you?" I asked.

"Yes, our meeting is scheduled for noon," Ms. Jackson answered.

"Okay, have a seat and I will let her know you are here," I said. *Ms. Deeds is not on campus today,* I thought. *I guess I can call her cell.*

"Hello," Ms. Deeds answered.

"Hey Ms. Deeds, did you have a meeting scheduled with Roy Jackson's mother at noon?"

"I sure did," she replied. "I need you to handle it for me, because I am at the hospital with my brother."

"What do you need me to say?"

"Just talk to them about Roy's behavior and discuss his last report card. Tell them Roy is going to be retained if he doesn't improve."

"Okay, I will handle it."

"Call me if you need to," she said, as she hurried off the phone.

I can't believe this. I'm supposed to threaten them with retention and I don't really know why. I quickly pulled his report card so I could have a sense of what I was dealing with.

"Ms. Jackson," I said, "I just spoke with Ms. Deeds. Unfortunately she had a family emergency and will not be able to meet with you. She asked that I sit in her place, if you don't mind."

By this time Roy had joined us in the office.

"No, I don't mind," she replied. "I just want to get to the bottom of this."

"Well, it seems that Roy's grades have taken a dramatic turn for the worst," I said. "He started the year fine, but it's been all downhill since. He's missed a lot of days as well."

"Mr. White, I am just going to be honest. I have been incarcerated since September and I was just released on bail last week. I told my mother to look after Roy, but I see she didn't," she said, turning to her mother, the elder Ms. Jackson, with a scowl marring her face. "So, why didn't you tell me Roy was missing school, Momma?"

The mother looked ashamed and mumbled, "I tried to do my best."

"Your best!" her daughter shouted. "You mean to tell me you couldn't make him go to school?" She then spent the next few minutes belittling her mother while Roy sat quietly.

I was stunned. I couldn't believe the daughter, who was just released from jail, was chastising her mother for the manner in which she had cared for her grandchild during her absence.

"You know what," the younger Ms. Jackson said, "We are going to discuss this at home. I am just tired of dealing with this. Roy, if you fail, it's your own fault." She returned her gaze to me. "Thank you, Mr. White, but I don't have any more time for this. I have my own problems to deal with." Saying no more, she left the office with the elder Ms. Jackson following sheepishly behind her.

"What are you going to do, Roy?" I asked him before he could slip out of the office.

"What do you mean?" he asked.

"Do you want to end up like your mother? That's exactly where you are headed if you keep this up."

Roy was a good kid, but I knew he had too many negative influences around him. His father was murdered when he was a baby and his mother was not the model citizen. His older brother was also on his way to a life of crime.

"You just don't understand, Mr. White," he said. "It's easy for you to judge me, because you don't have to go through what I have to. I have been criticized and judged all of my life. Teachers think I'm a bully because the other kids are scared of me. I never get picked for anything good. Everyone always assumes that I am doing something bad. I feel like if that's what you want, that's what I am going to give you."

Roy was big for his age. He had dark smooth skin to go with a muscular build. However, he still had the smile of a baby. He reminded me of my best friend who I had known since kindergarten. They were almost identical at that age. I knew the hardships my friend had endured as a child and as a man. Teachers would always compliment me and not him for being smart even though we made practically the same grades. As a teenager, the police would harass him and not me in shopping malls for no apparent reason. It was always assumed that he was up to no good, while I was encouraged to do well by my elders. I could empathize with Roy. I told him all about my friend and how he overcame all those obstacles and became a successful businessman.

"Roy, you can be greater than him," I said. "All you have to do is believe you can."

"I hear you, Mr. White," he said, and looked at me for a moment before he asked, "Can I go to class now?"

"Go ahead," I replied, "but we need to talk later."

A few weeks had passed since Ms. Lilly had left and we were getting used to her absence. Meanwhile, Mrs. Robinson and I were laying down the groundwork for starting our school.

"Good morning, Mr. White," she said as she strode into the office accompanied by another woman. "I would like you to meet Ms. Allwood. Ms. Deeds has decided to hire her to help you in the office."

"Well, that's great news," I exclaimed all smiles and standing up to greet the newcomer. "It's nice to meet you and welcome to the family." *When did this happen,* I thought.

"I am going to show her around campus and probably spend the rest of the week training her," Mrs. Robinson said.

"Hey, that's fine with me," I replied.

Suddenly, the door of the office burst open and in rushed a student. "Mr. White, Mr. White, we need you out back!" he yelled.

Not waiting for an explanation, I jumped to my feet and followed him. "What's going on?"

Before I got a response I could see Mr. Steel pace back and forth at the back of the campus. *The volcano has finally erupted,* I thought.

"Mr. Steel, is everything okay?" I asked.

"No, no it's not, Mr. White," he replied. "I've messed up. I've messed up really bad this time."

I could see the anguish and regret in his face.

"What happened?"

"I told Julius Little to sit down and stop talking, but he refused," he said. "The next thing I know, he came towards me and I pushed him. I really didn't mean to. He rushed up to me so fast I just reacted."

"Is he hurt?" I asked.

"I don't think so," he replied. "However, he did fall to the ground."

Julius Little was a big boy, so I'm sure the push didn't hurt. *But I am willing to bet falling to the ground didn't feel that good*, I thought.

"Okay, just get yourself together and I will sit with your class. Is Julius inside the classroom?"

"Yes, he's still in there. I just lost my cool, Mr. White."

"Don't worry about it," I said. "It happens."

He might as well kiss his job goodbye, I thought. Julius's mother was going to do everything within her power to get him fired.

When I walked into the classroom, the rowdy students quickly dispersed back to their desks. I could see Julius close his cell phone as if he just ended a call. I was sure he had called his mother.

"Who can tell me what happened?" I asked.

Hands went up immediately.

"Mr. Steel pushed Julius for no reason and made him fall," one student yelled as the class began to laugh.

"Mr. Steel is crazy," said another student.

"What do you all know about Mr. Steel?" I asked. The kids looked confused by the question. "Did you know that Mr. Steel almost made it to the NFL? Did you know that he graduated with a B average in Economics?"

"Well, if he is so great, why is he working here?" blurted a student, causing the entire class to laugh.

"He is here because he wanted to help you," I answered.

Mr. Steel always spoke of how he wanted to help mentor students and share some of his experiences. Now his dream had become a nightmare. Just as I was about to lecture the students, Coach Robinson arrived.

"Mr. White, Ms. Deeds needs to see you in her office," he said. "I will watch the class."

You mean she is here today? Extraordinary!

"Thanks, Coach," I replied, walking out of the classroom. I could see the disappointment in Coach Robinson's eyes as I departed.

Ms. Deeds was just ending a phone conversation when I arrived in her office.

"Mr. White, I am going to fire Mr. Steel," she said casually. "He can't put his hands on the students and expect there be no consequences. I like him, but he's got to go."

"I understand," I replied.

"Did he admit to pushing the boy?" she asked.

"Yes. He admitted to pushing him."

"Well, I need you to write a statement detailing everything he told you just in case he tries to deny it. Did you meet Ms. Allwood?"

"Yes, Mrs. Robinson introduced us."

"Yes, I really like her," she said. "I met her at a party and she already has experience working in a school office. She should work out nicely."

"How's your brother?" I asked, purposely changing the subject.

"He's fine," she replied, confusion written all over her face. "Why do you ask?"

"I thought he was in the hospital," I said.

"Oh, oh, he's doing better," she muttered. "He is being released today."

145

I left Ms. Deeds's office more confused than before I arrived. I guess Mr. Steel doesn't get a chance to explain his side of the story and once again nothing was going to happen to the real culprit. Julius was going to be free to bully any teacher any time he wanted now – even though he may have charged Mr. Steel.

Ms. Allwood was in the office when I returned. "Where is Mrs. Robinson?" I asked.

"She had to leave abruptly," she said. "She mentioned being late for a meeting with the bus company. She told me to answer the phone and sit at the front desk."

"That's cool," I replied. "So how do you know Ms. Deeds?"

"That's an interesting question," she replied. "I actually date Ms. Deeds's ex-husband."

"Come again?" I was shocked.

"I know it sounds crazy, but there it is. Yet I should tell you that even though I am dating Ms. Deeds's ex-husband, we are pretty good friends. Our daughters even go to the same school."

"I guess mature adults can handle awkward situations," I suggested, still amazed at this new turn of events.

Interesting how Ms. Deeds said she met her at a party, I thought.

A few days had passed and Ms. Allwood turned out to be a great help around the office. She was very well organized which was something we really needed, especially since I was always running around like a chicken with its head cut off.

"Mr. White, Mr. White, I have some great news," Mrs. Robinson said as she rushed into the office. She was beaming with excitement. "Ms. Ebony and Ms. Lloyd have resigned."

"What?" I erupted, under Ms. Allwood's amazed gaze. "What happened?"

"Well, this past weekend the Dance instructor hit one of our students with a drumstick," Mrs. Robinson explained. "Ms. Ebony didn't report it to Ms. Deeds before the student's parents called. As a result, Ms. Deeds chewed her out. I guess Ms. Ebony felt disrespected, so she resigned. Ms. Lloyd just resigned because her sister did."

"Just like that, they are gone?" I asked. I couldn't be more dumbfounded. *This was turning out to be a real sitcom. This is a huge loss.* Even though I didn't agree with some of the things Ms. Ebony did, I still believed she was good for the kids. She seemed to care for them. The seventh grade girls loved her. *This is an enormous loss,* I repeated to myself.

"Mrs. Robinson, we are already operating with a skeleton crew," I said. "How are we going to cope with losing two more staff members?"

"I already have that covered," she replied. "I called Mr. Baxter from the bus company and he accepted a position with us. And, I have another teacher starting on Monday."

"Damn, Mrs. Robinson, you don't mess around," I said, smiling.

"That's right, Mr. White," she said. "Make sure you are doing your job, because I may have a replacement for you."

"I believe you would," I said, chuckling. I paused. "So when do I get to meet Mr. Baxter?"

"In about two hours. He is coming to complete his paperwork. The new teacher, Mr. Willis, will be here as well."

Both Mr. Baxter and Mr. Willis arrived exactly two hours later – punctuality seemed to be in their make-up, which was a good start, I thought. Even though I had not officially met them, I had seen both of them on campus before. Mr. Baxter had been to the campus for meetings regarding bussing matters since he was a manager with the bus company we used. Mr. Willis was actually friends with Mr. Holly and was helping with the step team.

"How are you, gentlemen?" I said as I greeted them. "I just want to welcome you to the family."

Mr. Baxter was a handsome man and dressed rather meticulously. Mr. Willis reminded me of Mr. Jackson. He sported the afro and dressed a little more hippish.

"Hello, gentlemen," Mrs. Robinson said as she entered the office. "I see you all have met Mr. White. I need you gentlemen to come with me. Ms. Deeds needs to speak with you. Also, Mr. White, Ms. Deeds needs to speak with you once school ends today."

"I see we've hired some more handsome men around here," Ms. Allwood said as they left the office. "Mrs. Robinson is doing such a great job."

I don't know if the fact that they're handsome will help them in fixing this mess, I thought.

The day was finally over and I couldn't wait to get this meeting with Ms. Deeds over so I could go home.

"Hey, Mr. White," she said as I entered her office. "What do you think about the new hires?"

"They seem alright so far," I said.

"Well, I have decided since Ms. Ebony and Ms. Lloyd resigned that I need to rid our school of all the trash. I am going to terminate Mr. Gordon. He hasn't shown any improvement, but has actually gotten worse. I have decided you are either with me or against me. There can be no in between."

"So when are you going to notify him?" I asked.

"He should be on his way to the office now," she replied. "That's why I needed you here. I don't know how he's going to take it."

What the hell, I thought. *He's going to think I am involved in this. This is a bunch of bull.* And just like clockwork, Mr. Gordon arrived.

"Hello, Ms. Deeds," he said as he entered. "Hey, Mr. White." He was visibly surprised to see me.

"Hello, Mr. Gordon," Ms. Deeds said. "Just have a seat next to White. I'm not going to beat around the bush. You know as well as I do that your performance has not improved. Unfortunately, I don't see you making any improvements before the school-year ends, so I have decided to let you go."

I could tell Mr. Gordon was taken aback by the announcement, but he almost seemed relieved.

"I understand," he replied. "I just want to thank you for the opportunity and I am sorry things didn't work out. If you don't mind, I can clean out my things this evening."

"No, of course I don't," Ms. Deeds said. "Just make sure you give your keys to White before you leave."

The entire conversation was brief and to the point. It seemed like I was the only one stunned by the news. *Maybe I'm just too sensitive,* I thought.

That evening, Mr. Gordon quickly gathered his things and gave me his keys.

"I hate to see you go," I said to him as he was leaving.

"It's cool, Mr. White, I was wondering when this was going to happen."

"You take it easy and good luck," I told him, shaking his hand.

And just like that he was gone.

I could not believe the high turnover that was happening. In a matter of a few months, we had lost five staff members. I couldn't wait for the end of the school year.

In the meantime, Mr. Baxter and Mr. Willis were fitting in well at the school. Mr. Baxter was handling all the daily operations and Mr. Willis was teaching very well.

"Good morning, Mr. White," Mr. Baxter said to me as I arrived into the office. "I need to speak with you for a moment."

"Sure, what's up?" I asked him, dropping my briefcase beside my desk.

"Ms. Deeds informed me that my hiring was not approved by Mr. Banker. Therefore, I am not officially an employee, which means that I am not going to receive any money for this upcoming pay period."

"What?" Needless to say I was astonished. "I thought Mrs. Robinson had taken care of all of that before you started."

He nodded. "I can't afford to miss a check. You see, I have a wife and four children. I don't work for free."

"Let me speak with Ms. Deeds," I said. "Give me some time."

I immediately called her.

"Hey, White," she said as she answered her phone.

"Ms. Deeds," I said without the usual preamble – I wasn't in the mood for chit-chat. "Mr. Baxter just told me about his situation."

"Yeah, Mrs. Robinson hired those guys without clearing it with Banker," she said, "now Banker's telling me that I can't pay them."

"So what are you going to do?"

"I don't know. I have been on the phone with human resources all morning trying to work this out. As a matter of fact, they are calling me now. I will call you back...."

I was shocked. How do you hire someone and then tell them they are not hired? Mr. Baxter was staring at me when I hung up the phone with Ms. Deeds.

"She's trying to work on it as we speak," I said, trying to reassure him.

I could see the worry on his face. "My rent is due this week. What am I supposed to tell my landlord?"

"How much do you need to carry you until this gets worked out?"

"I need my full pay."

"I know that. Give me a number."

"I need at least a thousand to cover rent and food."

"Let's do this. I can loan you the money until you get paid," I suggested.

"You would do that?" he asked, quite surprised by the gesture.

"I know where you work," I said. "I can get my money back."

A smile appeared on his lips. "Well apparently you know more than I do, because I thought I knew where I worked. I found out something different today. Trust me, I will pay you back. You are a good dude, Mr. White."

"I can give you the money tomorrow, but I will need you to sign a promissory note as well," I said.

"No problem. You know Mr. Willis isn't going to get paid as well?"

"Yeah, I figured as much," I replied.

The next day Mr. Baxter and I made the exchange and continued to work as if nothing had ever happened. Later that day Ms. Deeds approached me.

"Mr. Baxter told me what you did," she said. "I appreciate you bailing me out. I wish Mrs. Robinson hadn't jumped the gun on hiring them. Here is the money you gave Mr. Baxter," handing me an envelope. "I took some money out of my savings and paid Mr. Baxter and Mr. Willis. Hopefully, they will be approved before the next pay period."

"Have you seen Mrs. Robinson?" I asked her as she was about to leave.

She turned her head to me – something was wrong…. "She called in sick."

I wonder how Mrs. Robinson could have hired these guys without Ms. Deeds's permission, I thought. *I'm willing to bet Mrs. Robinson doesn't even know she is taking the blame for all of this. I can't wait to tell Regina about this.*

The next morning I travelled my usual route to work. I picked up Mr. Holly from the bus stop at the same time I always did. However, I wanted to test him, so I decided to stop for gas. I stopped at a gas station that had a McDonald's located on the inside.

"Are we stopping for breakfast, Boss?" he asked with excitement while grinning from ear to ear. "We never get breakfast in the morning."

"No, I just need to get some gas," I replied. "I am almost on empty."

"Oh," is all he said, visibly uncomfortable and perhaps a little dejected.

I slowly looked for my credit card trying to give him an opportunity to offer to pay for the gas. However, he turned his head and looked out the window without saying a word. *My test worked,* I thought. *This guy has been riding back and forth to work with me and has made no attempt to pay for gas. This will be his last ride.*

"Oh, by the way, Mr. Holly," I said when I finished filling up my tank, "I won't be able to continue giving you rides to work."

"Why not?" He threw me a baffled glare. Obviously he thought life was a free-for-all type of thing.

"I have to pick up Douglas from a different location now," I told him, climbing behind the wheel once again.

"His parents can't take him to school?" Mr. Holly asked with visible annoyance.

I looked at him and he quickly got the message before I could say anything.

"It's cool," he said. "I may be purchasing a vehicle this weekend anyway."

The nerve of this guy, I thought. I kept envisioning pushing him out of my truck while we were on the freeway. *Must think positively* is what I kept telling myself. Just as I was about to burst, my phone rang.

"Morning, Ms. Deeds," I said when I saw her number on the display screen.

"Mr. White, where are you?" She sounded frantic.

"I'm about ten minutes away from the school," I replied. "What's wrong?"

"I need you to call me back as soon as you get in the office," she urged.

"Okay. Give me a few minutes."

I wondered what could have happened this time. As I arrived at the school, I headed straight to the office and called her. "Ms. Deeds, I'm in the office, what's happened?"

"Is anyone around you?" she asked.

"No, I'm alone."

"Well, Mrs. Robinson and Coach Robinson had a big fight yesterday and I'm scared something bad may have happened…." I was stunned – to put it mildly. "Mrs. Robinson and I were talking on the phone when she arrived home last night and I could hear Coach yelling at her as she entered the doorway. I couldn't understand what he was saying, but he was extremely upset. The next thing I knew the phone went dead. I tried calling her back, but she wouldn't answer. I am really afraid for her, Mr. White."

"Have you tried calling her this morning?" I asked.

"Yes, but she didn't answer my call, although she did send me a text saying that she was going to be late."

"I don't know what to say, Ms. Deeds. I guess we should just wait and see if she comes in." I don't know if my voice sounded soothing enough, but there wasn't anything else we could do for the time being.

"You're right, but I am really worried," she said. "There has been quite a bit of turmoil going on with them for quite some time now. I will call you if I hear anything else."

I was surprised to hear Coach and Mrs. Robinson were having marital issues. They definitely put on a good show when they're at work. Oh well, I guess this is just another day at the school.

"Good morning, Mr. White," Mr. Baxter said when he arrived into the office.

"Good morning to you too," I replied.

"I can't thank you enough for helping me," he said. "I don't know many people who would do that. If you need anything, I'm here for you."

"Don't worry about it," I said. "I may need you to back me up today. Mrs. Robinson might not come in today."

"Is she okay?" he asked.

"I'm not sure. I think she may be a little under the weather. I will let you know when I hear something...." I left it at that and went to the cafeteria for breakfast duty.

All I could think about during breakfast was if Mrs. Robinson was okay. Ms. Deeds sounded fearful that her husband may have turned violent.

Just as breakfast was ending, my phone vibrated. It was a text from Ms. Deeds. It read, "Please come to my office in exactly thirty minutes". Something must really be wrong. *I wonder why she just didn't call me?* I waited exactly thirty minutes and headed straight to her office. As I got closer to her office I could see Coach Robinson coming towards me from Ms. Deeds's direction.

"What's up, Coach?" I asked him, acting as if I didn't know anything.

"Morning, White," he said rather coldly.

He then turned around and started walking with me towards Ms. Deeds's office.

"How was your weekend?" I asked, trying to make conversation.

"Not too good," he replied as we entered Ms. Deeds's office. And then, without a word of warning, he blasted at our principal. "Listen, either you setup a meeting or I will!"

"Okay, give me some time," Ms. Deeds replied sedately.

I could see Mrs. Robinson standing in a corner looking rather frail. I had never seen her look so afraid before. She was almost shaking.

"Let me know something by the end of the day!" Coach yelled, turning on his heels and slamming the office door on his way out.

"Mr. White…," Ms. Deeds said rather nonchalantly.

"Morning, ladies," I said acting as if I had not witnessed Coach Robinson's display.

"Mrs. Robinson, you need to stay home and take care of those sick kids you have," Ms. Deeds said as if we had not spoken earlier.

"Yes…, that's what I will do," she whispered, retreating carefully and walking out of Ms. Deeds's office.

"Mr. White, Mr. White," Ms. Deeds repeated as she took a seat. "You are not going to believe what happened."

"I'm all ears," I replied, sitting down across from her in one of the visitors' chairs.

"Mrs. Robinson was having an affair," she announced.

"What?" I felt like a ton of bricks had just hit me in the chest.

"I told her to watch herself." Ms. Deeds shook her head in dismay. "She just wouldn't listen."

I was dumbfounded. "With who?" I asked.

"One of our board members, Robert Wynans."

I knew Robert was visiting the campus quite often, but I actually thought it was Ms. Deeds who might have been involved with him.

"They have been messing around for quite some time," she went on. "Somehow Coach Robinson found out. Get this. Coach Robinson is demanding twenty thousand dollars from Robert not to tell his wife."

"What?" I exclaimed again. "That doesn't make sense. Besides, it sounds to me like blackmail."

"I know," Ms. Deeds nodded. "I spoke with Robert earlier and he believes this whole thing was a setup. He thinks Mrs. Robinson and Coach Robinson planned the whole thing."

This was truly unbelievable. First, I find out Mrs. Robinson is having an affair. Now, Ms. Deeds is saying she may be part of something even more sinister.

And yet that wasn't the end of this episode; "That's not even the whole story," she said. "Coach Robinson suspects that Robert is not the only person she's involved with. And I think he may be right."

I was speechless. The one person who I really trusted turns out to be just like everyone else.

"So what are we going to do?" I asked.

"Well, I have to let Banker know about this since Coach Robinson is demanding money. I will let you know what he says."

"Okay, I need to get back to the office…," I said, rising to my feet and walking out more baffled than ever.

My mind was racing out of control when I returned to the office.

"You okay, Mr. White," Mr. Baxter asked as soon as I sat at my desk.

"I'm good," I replied, not wanting to let the "cat out of the bag."

"Well, rumors are already circulating," he said. "Rumor has it Mrs. Robinson and Coach are having some issues."

I could tell he was fishing. "Well, Mr. Baxter, sometimes things aren't always as they seem. I could tell you some things that would blow your mind."

"Mr. White, I could tell you some things that would blow yours," he replied.

I could sense that he was hinting at something. "Maybe we need to swap stories."

"I think we should, Mr. White."

"Why don't we get some dinner after school today?"

"Sounds good to me."

Later that evening we met at a restaurant on the other side of town.

"Okay, Mr. Baxter, I'm all ears," I said.

"Well, for starters, tell me what happened with Mrs. Robinson," he asked. "And just so you know, I heard she was having an affair."

"That's correct," I replied. "Ms. Deeds told me she was having an affair with one of our board members and Coach found out. Ms. Deeds seems to think she's having an affair with someone else as well."

"That doesn't surprise me," Mr. Baxter said.

"Why is that?"

"Because Mrs. Robinson is not the person you think she is, Mr. White."

"What are you talking about?"

"Mrs. Robinson has been trying to sleep with me also."

"Really?"

"Yep, Mr. White, I am telling you this because I think you are a good guy and you deserve to know the truth. Mrs. Robinson has been trying to hire me since last year, but I didn't want to take the cut in salary. However, she assured me that it didn't matter how much my salary was. She was going to make sure I received the salary I wanted."

"And how was she going to do that?" I asked.

"She has access to the school's bank account. Do you not realize that she and Ms. Deeds use the school credit card as if it was their own? Why do you think Mrs. Robinson was always coming to my office when I worked for the bus company?"

"I thought she was viewing bus tapes," I said.

"Please, she wasn't coming for tapes," he said. "She used to buy me gifts all the time as well."

"Gifts?" I asked my astonishment unabated.

"Yes," he replied. "One day she met me at Barnes & Noble and paid for the books I was purchasing. I tried to stop her, but she said "the school needs books" as she gave the school credit card to the cashier."

"Why are you telling me this, Mr. Baxter?"

"Because she lied to me. Not only did I take a cut in pay coming here, but I'm still not officially an employee. Mr. Banker can tell me to leave at any time and I will have no job to go to. Basically I'm screwed."

"How do I know you are telling the truth?"

"You can look it up. Just check the credit card statements. She purchased those books for me in November. She also sent me a fruit bouquet in December. I'm pretty sure she used the credit card. Besides, I know things about her sexually as well. Would you be surprised if I told you she was bisexual?"

"Nothing really surprises me at this point, Mr. Baxter."

"She told me on several occasions that she could arrange a threesome with a really good friend of hers if I was interested," he said.

"With who? Ms. Deeds?"

"She never said who. She only said the person was a good friend of hers, but I don't think she was talking about Deeds."

"I guess you know more than I thought you did."

"Yep. However, I am telling you this because I trust you."

"Don't worry," I replied. "I won't say a thing. I do have one question and I will only ask this once. Did you sleep with her?"

"No," he replied without hesitation.

I knew he wasn't being truthful. I couldn't see Mrs. Robinson spoiling him with gifts and receiving nothing in return. But I understand why he couldn't answer truthfully as well. He had a wife and children that depended on him. We finished our dinner and headed home.

I couldn't wait to tell Regina about this. Mr. Baxter seemed like a good guy, but I realized then that he was not to be trusted. He didn't have good intentions from the beginning. If he expected Mrs. Robinson to give him money secretly, what else was he hoping to get?

As for me personally, I was devastated. Mrs. Robinson and I had made plans to open a new charter school. But now, there was no way on earth that I would associate my name and reputation with a woman who would have been suspected of collusion, fraud and extortion. I felt as if my dream and purpose had been shattered in the space of the last twenty-four hours. Even if all of these nasty rumors and innuendoes proved untrue or exaggerated, I would not risk opening a school with Mrs. Robinson at this juncture. Thinking about what had occurred during the last few months since she had begun working in the office with me, I could see a pattern developing before my eyes. She was always out for one meeting or another; she bought expensive lunches; her apparels were invariably fashionable and she never seemed to have time for the mundane things that we had to deal with on a day to day basis.

The next day the mood on campus was strange. It was obvious the news of Mrs. Robinson's affair had spread among the teachers, but everyone behaved as if they did not know.

"Mr. White," Ms. Deeds called, "I need you to come to my office as soon as possible. We need to get on a conference call with Banker."

"No problem," I replied. "I am on my way now."

When I arrived at her office, she was already on the phone with Banker.

"Amber, this is the type of nonsense we don't need on your campus," Banker was saying. "Did you not know this was happening?"

"How could I?" she replied. "Mrs. Robinson is an adult and I don't know what she is doing when she's not at work."

"Let's be clear," Banker said, "this affair has nothing to do with us. However, I think this is a major distraction. Who is more important to you, Mr. or Mrs. Robinson?"

Ms. Deeds paused and then replied, "Coach Robinson."

I was astonished by her response, because I thought they were really close friends. However disgraceful or in doubt her behavior had been, Mrs. Robinson had done so much to support her and this was how she was repaid?

"Great, then either fire Mrs. Robinson or find another school willing to take her," Banker stated. "Do you have any other staff members that have close relationships outside of school?"

Again Ms. Deeds paused then answered, "No."

That's not true, I thought. *Ms. Allwood is your ex-husband's girlfriend. Mr. Anderson is Mrs. Robinson's brother. I'm pretty sure you know about Mrs. Robinson's infatuation with Mr. Baxter. Lastly, you were having an affair with Mr. Jackson.* I wanted to tell Banker everything I knew, but for some reason I couldn't. I didn't want the school to fail because of the poor decisions made by a few people. I left Ms. Deeds's office more conflicted than I had ever been.

"Mr. White," I heard someone yell as I was leaving. It was Mrs. Gillis.

"Hey Mrs. Gillis," I replied as I turned towards her direction.

"I really need to speak with you, Mr. White."

"What's up," I said as I walked into her empty classroom.

"I know you heard about Mrs. Robinson and Robert?" she inquired.

"You know too?" I responded.

"Of course I do," she replied. "He used to meet up with Mrs. Robinson and me when we would go to Happy Hour."

"Why didn't you say anything?"

"It's not my place to tell adults what they should and shouldn't do. Besides this wasn't the first time."

"What do you mean?"

161

"Mr. White, you can't be this naïve! Mrs. Robinson has been plotting to sleep with you."

"WHAT!"

"Don't act like you didn't know she liked you. Why do you think she wanted you to work here? She's been after you from the day she received your resume for Saturday school."

"How do you know all of this?"

"She told me about you a long time ago."

So this means you two knew each other before you started working here, I thought.

"Mrs. Robinson remembered you from high school. She said all the girls knew who Jacoby White was. She was surprised you didn't remember her."

"I still don't remember her from school."

"She was a short-haired Tomboy back then. Now she's a diva," she said with a smile. "It was Mrs. Robinson's idea to move you into the office so she and you could work closely together. You need to get your head out of the clouds and pay attention to what's really going on around you. Mr. White, I am telling you this in the strictest of confidence."

"I'm listening."

"Coach Robinson told me one day Mrs. Robinson asked him hypothetically if he had a choice, which teacher on this campus would he like to sleep with. He said me."

"Okay...." I said slowly.

"He then asked her the same question and she said me as well."

"Whoa, you are lying," I said flabbergasted.

"No, I'm not," she said laughing. "If you think that's bad, you are not going to believe this. Coach Robinson tried to rape me."

"What! What do you mean he tried to rape you?" I couldn't believe what I was hearing and how casually she said it.

"He tried to rape me. We were in his classroom one evening and he grabbed me. Before I knew it he pulled my shorts down to my ankles."

"Wait a minute. This doesn't make sense. He just out of the blue grabbed you and pulled your pants down?"

"Yes! I pushed him away and left his office."

I couldn't believe Coach Robinson did this. He never seemed like the type, but I guess they rarely do. However, Mrs. Gillis did not seem upset at all. She actually behaved as if it was sort of funny.

"So are you sure you didn't do anything that made him think it was okay to pull your pants down?"

"No, I didn't do anything. It happened so fast, I couldn't do or say much of anything outside of leaving."

The kids were starting to gather outside of Mrs. Gillis's classroom because it was time for her next class.

"Let's talk about this later Mrs. Gillis."

"Sure, but before you leave read this text he sent me after it happened," she said as she handed me her phone.

The text clearly stated it was from Coach Robinson and read, "I apologize for what happened. However, were you afraid of getting caught or afraid you couldn't handle it?"

"I'm telling you the truth Mr. White."

"This is just too much," I replied as I left her classroom.

I still don't know if I believe it was attempted rape, I thought. I think she would've reported him if she wasn't a willing participant. More than likely they were messing around and he wanted to take it to the next level. She on the other hand realized a classroom was not an ideal place to do it

163

which is why she resisted. And I was just feeling really bad for Coach in regards to Mrs. Robinson's affair. It seems he was busy himself. Now I know I can't trust Mrs. Gillis as well. *Why was she so willing to tell me those stories? Was she testing me?* I learned a valuable lesson that day. *There is no honor amongst thieves.*

Discovery

The time had come for me to comb through our financial records. I couldn't put it off any longer. Mr. Baxter said some things that really made me question how the school's money was being spent. I started by reviewing the school budget. The budget was done in Microsoft Excel so it wasn't very difficult to follow. The first tab, labeled "Enrollment", was used to enter the projected number of students for each grade level. This was the most important aspect of the budget because the number of students enrolled determined the amount of money we received from the state. We received approximately $6,000 for each child as long as we maintained a 98% attendance rate. Now, I understood why attendance was so important. Anytime a student missed school, we lose money. I also noticed some additional columns that seemed peculiar. There were columns for projecting the number of students labeled as Special Education, LEP (Limited English Proficient) and Free/Reduced Lunch. It seemed that we received additional funds for each student who had one or more of these labels. This explained why schools were quick to attach a learning disability tag on a student. This also explained why parents are encouraged to apply for free or reduced lunch. It amazed me how so many students were receiving these benefits without their parents having to prove their income. It was almost frowned upon to even question the validity of their applications. The next tab was labeled "Payroll". This tab listed the entire staff along with their salaries. In the education industry, your years of experience directly correlated with the amount of money you made. At least that was what I was told. It was obvious I had been deceived. All first year teachers, including me, were paid the same. So I expected our salaries to be the lowest. However, Mr. Jackson, who was a first year teacher, was being paid much more. *It seems that having an affair with Ms. Deeds has its benefits.* I also noticed that Mrs. Robinson was one of the highest paid staff members even though several other teachers had more years of experience. Coach Robinson's salary was higher than at least half of the staff and he didn't even have a degree. The most appalling salary was Ms. Deeds's. As a principal she made over six figures which I personally believed the position deserved. However, she wasn't fulfilling the requirements of the position. The next tab was labeled "Operating Data Entry". This tab detailed how Ms. Deeds planned to spend the remaining money not used for payroll. Most of the expenses were operational costs. However, some of them looked a little peculiar. For example, 20k was budgeted for office furniture even though all the furniture we had had been donated. There were several items budgeted as "other" that totaled about 50k. There was another section for "instruction supplies". It was given a budget of 36k. I couldn't believe this. We were told there was no money in the budget for supplies. There was 10k allocated for student rewards. However, I never saw any rewards handed out. There was 7k allocated for the student store. We didn't have a student store. This just blew me away. Next, I needed to look at the credit card accounts. Ms. Deeds, Mrs. Robinson and Mr. Baxter were all given credit cards so it was easy to see who was misusing school funds. *Mr. Baxter has not been with us that long, so he shouldn't have too many charges,* I thought. Boy was I wrong. There were numerous charges for food and gas on his card. Since the credit card was for the school, he had to add a short explanation for each charge in the accounting system. He actually stated that each charge for gas was for having to use his personal vehicle. We rarely used our vehicles for business reasons. Hell, we never had the time to leave the campus. However, he was filling up his gas tank every week using the credit card. He also had numerous charges for food that he stated was for faculty lunches. I am sure the other teachers would've liked to have been invited to some of these lunches. I don't think six dollars at Chick-Fil-A would feed an entire staff. *Yep, Mr. Baxter is just as dirty as they are,* I thought. I wondered what Mrs. Robinson had on her card. Mr. Baxter already told me that she spent money on gifts for him. *Let's see if she really purchased an edible bouquet for him in December.* He was telling the truth. She purchased an edible arrangement for $80 and labeled it as a "gift of appreciation". As a matter of fact, she purchased several edible arrangements throughout the year, totaling $400. I guess Mr. Baxter wasn't the only one receiving gifts. It also appeared she was using her personal vehicle for school business quite often as well. She was purchasing gas almost every week like Mr. Baxter did. From reviewing her charges, it was easy to see what her favorite restaurants were. Pappadeaux's Seafood Kitchen and Luby's Café showed up repeatedly. The charges that really threw me for a loop were the ones at various grocery stores. *How can she justify the numerous purchases at Krogers, Target and Wal-Mart? There is no way this is for the school.* Finally, I got to Ms. Deeds's charges. She had the same type of charges as Mr. Baxter and Mrs. Robinson did, times three. It seemed that she ate out almost every other night. There had been a rumor that she paid for Mr. Jackson to get his teacher certification even though I was told each teacher had to pay for their own. And what did my eyes see? A $1500 charge for ACT Houston which is a teacher certification program. She even stated in the description that this was for Mr. Jackson. I wondered if she charged the trip she took with Mr. Jackson to New Orleans. Yep, she sure did! There was a charge for the car rental and hotel.

There were also several charges for various restaurants where they dined. She charged just under $1300 for that entire trip. *I wonder if Ms. Deeds purchased that suit Mr. Jackson wore for the inauguration.* And there it was! She spent $370 at K&G Menswear and labeled it as a student gift. It seemed to me that Mr. Jackson was a kept man. I then understood why she was getting a divorce. Apparently she had no qualms about being indiscreet with her purchases. She bought an entire bedroom set and labeled it as school furniture! *How could she do that?* Her total lack of scruples was beyond my understanding. The students' money was squandered away liberally on personal items – nothing more personal than bedroom furniture – while they were sharing old tables and desks that had seen the worst of wear through years of abuse. I was disgusted, to put it mildly. She also purchased over $1600 worth of electronics from Fry's Electronic store and labeled it as "instructional supplies". Our teachers didn't have anything high tech in their classrooms. I could not believe no one had said anything about this. *I'm sure someone in the accounting department has reviewed these charges.* Every time the school paid for something we had to provide a receipt to accounting along with an explanation as to the reason for the purchase. How could they not see this when it's right in front of their eyes? I needed to speak with Shirley in accounting. Maybe she could shed some light on how Ms. Deeds could get away with making these purchases.

The rest of the week seemed like a blur to me. Everything I had believed to be true turned out to be nothing but pure manipulation. I had a meeting scheduled with Mr. Banker on Monday afternoon, but I also wanted to meet with Shirley before I met with him.

"Mr. Baxter," I said, "I need you to cover for me because I have a budget meeting with Mr. Banker at 1:00 pm today."

"Sure," he replied, "is everything alright?"

"Oh yes, we just need to discuss next year's budget. If you see Ms. Deeds, let her know where I am."

"No problem."

I couldn't drive fast enough to the corporate office. I really wanted to speak with Shirley before my meeting with Mr. Banker. *I hope she doesn't leave for lunch.* I parked my car in the first available spot and dashed across the lawn, rushing to her office. She was just about to close her office door for lunch when I arrived.

"Hey, Shirley," I yelled as if I was surprised to see her.

"Hey, Mr. White. What brings you around this part of town?"

"Oh, I have a meeting with Mr. Banker," I said. "I'm a little early so I just wanted to drop by and say hello."

Shirley had been helping me a lot with balancing our budget and cleaning up some of Ms. Deeds's mess, so I felt I could trust her.

"How's it going?" I asked to break the ice.

"I can't complain," she said. "It's just been extremely busy. How's the budgeting going?"

"It's going…." I paused. "Shirley, I need to ask you a question about spending."

"Sure, what's up?" She turned from the door and invited me to come in. "Why don't you have a seat," she offered.

We both sat down – she behind her desk, me in the visitor's chair facing her.

I put my briefcase beside the chair and asked, "What is considered a justifiable expenditure?"

She shook her head. "Well, your principal has the authority to spend money on whatever she feels will benefit the school as long as it is aligned with what was allocated in the budget," she replied.

"So, what about charging dinners at expensive restaurants?"

"It depends. If she was handling school business then it's justifiable."

"What if she purchases clothing?"

"Well, is she purchasing it for a school related function?"

Shirley knew what I was insinuating, but she played along with me.

She fixed her gaze on me. "Jacoby, school leaders are given what we call "the power to lead". Now, of course, we don't want this to be abused which is why we try to put responsible people in place."

"So, if she wanted to purchase a car, it would be allowed if it was used for school functions," I said sarcastically.

"I think purchasing a car would raise a few red flags," she giggled.

"Okay. Thanks Shirley. I need to get to my meeting with Mr. Banker."

"Let me know if you have any more questions or concerns," Shirley said as I got up from the chair and walked out of her office.

Help the leader!

The power to lead, I thought. What happened to checks and balances? Ms. Deeds may not have purchased a vehicle, but she did buy a queen sized bedroom set. I found it hard to believe that no one noticed this when she actually turned in the receipt which said exactly what was purchased.

Mr. Banker was waiting in the conference room near his office when I arrived.

"How are you, Mr. White?" he said as I walked in.

"I am doing great. How about yourself?" I asked in turn, shaking his extended hand.

"The kids are well," he said. "When the kids are well, I'm well." He pointed to two of the chairs at the table. "Have a seat and let's talk about the budget. What were you able to find?"

I took a seat to his right and hesitated for a fraction of a second before I asked, "Do you want to talk about this coming year's budget or this past year?"

"Hum…, what I really would like to know is how did we end up 150k over budget for the past two years?"

Do I really want to blow the lid off this whole thing? Maybe I can just steer him to what I found. "Well, one issue I found that explains a big portion of the loss was Ms. Deeds's omission of two teachers on the payroll."

"What do you mean?" His eyebrows shot up.

"If you look at the list of teachers on the budget, you will see two are missing. This accounts for at least 100k of the 150k."

"You mean to tell me no one caught this?" He fixed his gaze on me. "Why didn't she notice two teachers were missing from the budget?"

Well, if you would've hired someone with just a small amount of business knowledge this would not have happened, I thought. *Or, maybe if someone in accounting would have reviewed it.*

"So what else did you find?" he asked.

I shook my head and opened the folder I had brought with me. "It just seems too much money is being spent on unnecessary things."

"Like what?"

"It seems we spent a great deal of money on food."

"What else?"

"We also spent heavily on trips."

"What trips are you talking about?"

"Well, I found several trips, some to New Orleans, Chicago, and Louisville," I replied. "I don't know the reasons for the trips, however."

I was trying to bait him into digging further, but he didn't say a word. I was surprised that he didn't question the food purchases or the trips.

"Another item I noticed was "other"," I said. "What is "other" used for? Ms. Deeds placed a great deal of her small purchases under the "other" category."

"Mr. White, I think we found the reason for Ms. Deeds's budget problem," Mr. Banker said. "If she had not forgotten those two teachers, we would not be meeting right now."

Wait, I thought. *Is he trying to end our meeting? I have to say something.* "Mr. Banker, we need to talk about what has been happening at the school."

"Sure, what's on your mind?" he asked.

"We can't continue to operate the same way. Ms. Deeds is not leading us in the right direction." I felt relieved to have said it to him, finally.

"What do you mean, Mr. White?" he asked, obviously challenging my introduction into the subject of misspending school funds.

"I mean, she is not consistent. She lacks structure which results in the school not having any structure. Also, she is not trustworthy."

Mr. Banker sat back in his chair with a grin. "Do you know how long I have been saying that? I couldn't agree with you more, Mr. White."

If you agree with me, then why is she still the principal? I thought.

"I have had several conversations with Ms. Deeds and we are trying to correct this problem. Right now Ms. Deeds is a good leader. I am trying to make her great. Mr. White, we need to help her."

We do not need to help her. We need to help the kids, I thought. *I could care less about helping her.*

"I appreciate you for coming to me with your concerns," Mr. Banker said. "It lets me know that we have some level of trust. Have you tried to speak with Ms. Deeds about your concerns?"

What is there to discuss, I thought. *Hey, Ms. Deeds, can we talk about the stealing you've been doing?* I don't think that conversation would go over too well.

"No, I haven't spoken with her," I replied.

"That's part of the problem, Mr. White. She can't correct the problem if she doesn't know it exists."

"Mr. Banker, it's obvious there are multiple problems with the way she is running the school."

"It's obvious to you and me," he said, "but maybe not to her. This is what I need you to do, Mr. White. Each time Ms. Deeds does something that's questionable; I need you to document it. I also want you to document

your response. We must help Ms. Deeds become a better school leader."
He rose from his chair. "Let's talk about this again next Friday. We can
discuss any items you've added to your list by then as well. Keep up the
good fight," he concluded as he patted me on the back.

What the hell just happened? I thought. I felt like he just patted me on
the ass and said "now leave and be a good boy." Did he not understand
what I was trying to tell him? If he knows how she is why does she still
have a job? Our sister school started the same time as our school, but they
are on their third school leader now. He didn't have a problem firing them,
so why is he keeping Ms. Deeds?

The drive home was strange. I didn't listen to any music, just my
thoughts. *I can't wait to tell Regina about this.*

In my opinion, one of the first virtues or qualities anyone involved in
the education of children should demonstrate is integrity. Ms. Deeds didn't
have any as far as I could tell. Going out to expensive restaurants, buying
suits for her lover-boy and bedroom sets instead of spending those
allocated funds on kids supplies or school furniture did not amount to
much display of integrity. Besides, Ms. Deeds wasn't the "school leader"
Mr. Banker seemed to think she was. Her decisions were all partial to her
interests – not designed to improve the well-being of any of the children.
None of the teachers initially employed at our school, who had resigned or
who had been fired, needn't have been if educational rules or simple
common sense had been applied.

If Mr. Banker was half the man everyone purported him to be, what
was he thinking when he wanted me to "help Ms. Deeds in becoming a
better school leader"? If he truly thought that she wasn't trustworthy, why
was he encouraging me to show her the path to proper leadership? It made
absolutely no sense to me.

Lastly, when it came to "reporting" every single thing Ms. Deeds did (or didn't do and should have done) to Mr. Banker, it felt as if he was asking me to spy on her. *Wait a minute; come to think of it, that's exactly what he wanted me to do!* And if he asked me to show her the proper way to handle matters, wasn't he also testing my ability to "guide" and "mentor" his "would-be leader"? And what would happen to me after I would have done all the mentoring? Ms. Deeds would remain in her position – the wrong one for her – and I would be left marooned behind my desk, taking the heat.

Too much stress

The week flew by and Monday was here again. I walked around campus like a zombie. As expected, Ms. Deeds was not around. I couldn't help but wonder if Mr. Banker told her what I said. However, I really didn't care.

Suddenly I felt my phone vibrate. "Hello…."

"Mr. White, this is Michelle. I need you to send the attendance in as soon as possible. You are well past your deadline."

"Yes, yes, I'm sorry, Michelle. I will get it to you right now. I am headed to my office as we speak and I just need to enter one more class." I hadn't even looked at today's attendance.

"Mr. White, why is it so difficult to get the attendance done on time? You are the only school that consistently misses the deadline."

"Again, Michelle, I apologize. You will have it in 10 minutes."

"I expect a phone call from you in 10 minutes telling me that you are done," she demanded.

"You got it…." I hung up feeling frustrated – and the day hadn't even begun yet.

It was going to take me at least three minutes to get to my office since I was on the other side of the campus, so I broke into a run.

"Mr. White, Mr. White, I need your help!" Ms. Hollins screamed as I rushed past her classroom.

"Not now, Mrs. Hollins," I said gruffly. "I will be back in 15 minutes."

"Yes, now, Mr. White!" she shouted. "Marvin and Rico are fighting!"

I had to make a quick u-turn into her classroom. The kids were yelling and screaming while Marvin and Rico were knocking over desks and destroying the classroom.

"Hey!" I screamed, "Shut up and sit down!"

The room fell silent. I grabbed both boys by their arms and rushed to my office.

"Sit down and I better not hear one word!" I ordered as we went inside.

"But he hit me first!" Marvin yelled.

"HEY!" I shouted. "I said no talking!"

"Ms. Deeds has been calling for you," Mr. Baxter said once the kids had settled down somewhat. "She needs you to call her as soon as possible."

I ran into my office and shut the door. I immediately scanned the attendance sheets and entered the absences for the day. I entered the last name and pressed the "Enter" button. *Done!* I thought. I looked at the clock and 10 minutes was actually 30. I couldn't believe it. With great reluctance, I called Michelle.

"Hello, Mr. White," she answered.

"You should have the attendance now. I would've called you earlier but I received a call from a parent right before I called you," I lied.

"That's okay, Mr. White. I just sent an email to Mr. Banker requesting another meeting to discuss your difficulties with processing the attendance. You should be receiving a call from him shortly."

If I could have reached through the phone line and choked her, I would have.

"Okay," I replied. "That's fine with me."

I sat back in my chair, took a deep breath and stared at the wall. I was still staring at it thirty minutes later when Mr. Baxter knocked on my door.

177

"Mr. White, what do you want to do with our two fighters?" he asked.

"Call their parents and tell them they are suspended for three days. Tell them I need to discuss withdrawing them as well before they are expelled."

"Are you okay?" He must have seen the stress in my face.

"I'm just tired of this mess. I think I may be getting sick."

"I understand. Don't forget to call Ms. Deeds."

"Thanks for reminding me. I will give her a call now."

"Hello, Ms. Deeds," I said as she answered her phone.

"Good morning, Mr. White. Listen, I will be out today. My brother had to be rushed to the hospital last night. When you get a chance I need you to make a deposit today. Last night I placed some candy money in the bottom drawer of your desk. I would have deposited it myself but I didn't have a chance to do so. You may need to count it as well."

I opened the drawer and there it was. Two large envelopes filled with money. Anyone could have stolen this.

"Okay, I will take care of it," I said, exhaling a sigh of relief mixed. *How can she be so irresponsible? If the money had been taken, I would have been blamed for its disappearance.*

"Great!" she replied. "Call me if you need anything."

Yeah right, I thought as I hung up the phone. It took me over an hour to prepare the deposit. Each denomination had to be counted and recorded. The deposit slip had to show the actual number of one dollar bills, five dollar bills, quarters, etc. I tallied a total of over 12 thousand dollars. *What has she been doing with all this money?*

Just as I was finishing, Mr. Baxter knocked on my door. "Mr. White, it's time for lunch…" He looked down at the stacks of bills on my desk. "Whoa! How much money is that?"

"It's about 12 thousand dollars," I answered indifferently.

"Where did you get that from?"

"This is the candy money Ms. Deeds has been keeping." I tried averting my gaze from his devious grin as he gazed at the money.

"Mr. White, it's a good thing you are the one depositing that. I don't think all of that money would make it to the bank if someone else had to do it."

"I hear you," I replied without looking at him. I understood what he was saying. I also realize he was testing me. "Listen. I need you to take care of lunch for me. I have to get this money to the bank."

"No problem. I got your back," he said, walking out of my office. "Oh, by the way," he said as he returned to my office. "I think I know who Mrs. Robinson was referring to when she proposed a threesome."

"Let me guess," I said. "Mrs. Gillis?"

"Yeah, how did you know?" he asked.

"Lucky guess."

"Well you are a good guesser. She's been making a few suggestive comments to me lately. I'm more than positive that she's the person Mrs. Robinson was referring to."

"Oh well Mr. Baxter, you better watch yourself."

"Don't worry, I know how to protect myself," he said with a grin as he departed. *This place is one big soap opera*, I thought.

Making large deposits such as this one was not a quick process. I had to be escorted into a private room with a money counter and the bank representative had to recount and document all the money I was depositing. As we were finally finishing, I received a call from one of my fifth grade parents.

"Hello, Mr. White."

"Hello, Mrs. Frazier, how are you?"

"I need you to tell my daughter not to get on the school bus. My husband will be picking her up."

"Okay, Mrs. Frazier. I am not on campus right now, but I will call the office and notify them."

"Thanks, Mr. White," she said.

I really liked Mr. and Mrs. Frazier. They were good parents. I called the office, but no one answered. I tried a few of the fifth grade teachers but they didn't answer either. School was about to release, so I knew I had to contact someone quickly. I sent a text to all the staff telling them not to allow Mrs. Frazier's daughter to ride the bus. I continued to call while I was driving back to campus when I was finally able to get Mr. Baxter.

"Mr. Baxter," I said, "Did you get my text regarding Lea Frazier?"

"No, why?"

"I sent a text stating not to allow her to ride the bus."

"I personally put her on the bus. She asked me which bus she was assigned to and took her to the right one. I even told the bus driver exactly where she was to be dropped off."

"Damn, Mr. Baxter, her father is on his way to pick her up," I blasted on the phone. "She doesn't know how to catch the bus. I need you to call dispatch and locate the bus she is on."

"Okay, I'll call right now." He sounded quite concerned by this time.

I could tell this was not going to end well. The campus was practically empty when I arrived back.

"Mr. White, Mr. White," said Shelley, a sixth grader.

"Shelley, why are you still here?"

"I missed my bus."

"Come with me to the office so we can call your mother," I said as I rushed to find Mr. Baxter.

He was just hanging up his phone when I walked in. His expression said it all. "Mr. White, we have a problem. Mr. Frazier just left and he is pissed."

Mr. Frazier was a big, intimidating guy, so I could only imagine what him being pissed looked like.

"Where did he go?" I asked.

"He went to look for his daughter," Mr. Baxter replied. "I called dispatch and the bus driver said Lea had been dropped off already. However, she didn't get off at the right stop."

"What?" I shouted. "How did that happen?"

"I don't know. I specifically told the bus driver what stop she was to get off."

I could feel my stomach drop. I could only imagine the pain her father was feeling. I immediately called him. He didn't answer, so I called Mrs. Frazier. She was still at work, but I could tell she had been crying.

"Mr. White, what happened?" she asked. "I thought you said you were going to make sure she didn't get on that bus." I could feel her anxiety through the phone. And I could feel my eyes start to water.

"I'm so sorry, Mrs. Frazier," I said as calmly as I could. "I tried to call your husband, but he didn't answer."

"No, no, do not call him. He is extremely upset. I don't know what he may do."

"Okay, I am heading to your neighborhood now. We will find her."

Within minutes, Mr. Baxter and I rushed out in separate vehicles to find Lea. The police had been notified as well. We combed that entire area. Mr. Baxter and I would call each other periodically for updates. I couldn't believe what was happening. I was trying not to think the worst. Each street I traveled I would see a group of children walking but Lea wasn't among them.

My phone rang. It was Mr. Baxter.

"Did you find her?" I asked.

"No, I was just about ask you the same question." Mr. Baxter replied.

"Okay, call me if anything changes," I said.

My phone rang. It was Ms. Deeds.

"Hey, Mr. White, I heard we have a student missing," she said.

"Yes, but we will find her," I replied.

"Keep me posted," she said before hanging up.

My phone rang again. This time it was Mrs. Frazier.

"Mr. White, my husband has Lea," she practically screamed over the line – so elated she was.

"Thank God!" I shouted. "Where was she?"

"It seems a woman saw her wandering the streets and asked her if she needed some help. Lea was able to give her our address, so she brought her to our house. My husband happened to pass by and saw them."

"Thank God," I said again with relief. "Can you please tell your husband that I would like to apologize to him?"

"I will tell him for you, Mr. White. I don't think you want to talk to him right now."

I felt so bad. I really wanted to speak with Mr. Frazier, because I needed him to know how sorry I truly was. When we returned to the office, Mr. Baxter kept talking about how the parents were to blame.

"They should not have waited until the end of the day to call us," he said. "We have 300 kids to monitor. They should've at least told her the correct stop."

I didn't say anything, because I was at a loss for words. Shelley was still in the office as well.

"Shelley, did you call your mother?" I asked.

"Yes, but she's still at work. She wants to know if you can take me home."

I looked at her, not trying to show my displeasure. "Grab your bag and let's go."

When we arrived at her home, Shelley's aunt was there waiting.

"Hey, Mr. White," she said. "Thanks for bringing Shelley home."

"No problem," I said.

"You know, Mr. White, Shelley and her mom really like the school. We think you are doing a great job."

"Thanks." I didn't really believe what she said.

"However, there are some parents considering withdrawing their kids," she said. "They don't like some of the teachers and they don't trust Ms. Deeds. I tried to tell them to give you guys a chance. This is still much better than the school district."

I don't know if that's really true anymore, I thought. "If I were you, I would withdraw my child as well" is what I really wanted to tell her. "We are trying our best," I uttered instead.

I drove home that evening more conflicted than I had ever been. Were we really trying our best? I do believe some of us were. Unfortunately, some of our leaders were not. That night after taking my shower, I just stared at myself in the mirror. *I looked different. I have aged considerably. I have bags and dark circles around my eyes. My hairline seems to have receded even further. I have more gray hairs than I remember. My body looks different. I have lost over 20lbs. since I started working for the school. I looked skinny and sick. My skin looked different too. I don't eat that much because I don't have much of an appetite. I don't sleep as much because of the long hours at work. My mother passed away at an early age from cancer and I truly believe her illness was brought on by stress. I cannot allow myself to have the same fate. I need to see a doctor.*

The time has come

The rest of the week seemed to have gone by unnoticed and before I knew it Friday had arrived. Friday was the day Mr. Banker and I were going to continue our conversation about Ms. Deeds. Just as I expected, he called me at 9:00 am on the dot.

"Hello, Mr. Banker," I said as I answered my phone. "How are you?"

"I'm well, Mr. White," he replied. "How's that list coming along?"

"I haven't started on the list yet."

"Mr. White, how are we going to help Ms. Deeds improve if we don't do the simple things?"

"Honestly, I don't see the purpose of the list. Ms. Deeds is an adult. She is not going to change, because she likes who she is."

"I couldn't disagree with you more," Mr. Banker said. "This whole situation is fixable. Ms. Deeds just needs help."

"The problem is we don't have time to wait for Ms. Deeds. We need to help the kids, not her."

"Mr. White, it sounds like you may have checked out."

"I checked out on her a long time ago," I said. "But I have not checked out on the kids."

"Mr. White, let me show you how to deal with a boss like Ms. Deeds," he said.

"Mr. Banker, this isn't my first job," I snapped. "I know how to deal with difficult bosses. I don't need to be coached."

"I'm not questioning your intelligence, but you are wrong. Mr. White, this is a learning tool that will help you when you become a school leader."

"Actually, it's not. I don't want to be a school leader. All I wanted to do was help the kids. That's it."

"Let's schedule another meeting to discuss this further. I have another call in five minutes, but I would like to continue this conversation. I still want you to start on that list as well."

"Okay, let me know when you want to meet," I replied.

I don't know what he is expecting, but I'm not going to create that list. This is ridiculous. I think it is time to check out. Thank God it's the weekend.

As usual the weekend flew by and I just couldn't see going in on Monday. I decided to call in sick.

That was the best Monday I had had in quite some time. It was so relaxing that I decided to call in on Tuesday. As expected, my phone never stopped ringing, but I decided not to answer it. I felt great. Spending time with my family was fantastic. Taking my daughter to school felt great. This is what life was like before this soap opera. I missed this part of my life. I decided to send Ms. Deeds an email stating that I needed to take the entire week off. She didn't respond or question it. I was surprised, but I think she knew I was done. The next Sunday arrived and again I did not want to return to work the following Monday. However, this time I felt I was never going back.

I wrestled with the idea of resigning the entire day. At 8:30pm I had made my decision. I was not going back. I decided to cut all ties effective immediately. I had a key to the building so I decided to return all of my things that night. Surprisingly, two teachers were there prepping their classrooms for the next day.

"Hey, Mr. White," Mrs. Dee said with a big grin on her face, "What are you doing here at this hour?"

"I should be asking you the same question," I replied. "I just need to drop off a few things. Can you do me a favor?"

"Sure," she said, looking at me in puzzlement.

"Can you give these keys to Mr. Baxter in the morning?"

"No problem. Everything okay?"

"Oh yeah, I couldn't be better," I replied with a big smile crossing my lips.

When I gave her those keys I felt like the shackles had been removed. I felt free. I returned home and gave my wife the biggest hug. I then grabbed my laptop and typed my letter of resignation.

Ms. Deeds –

It is with great sorrow that I am hereby tendering my resignation to you. Please accept this letter as formal notification that I am leaving my position. I have decided to return to the Oil & Gas industry.

This resignation is effective immediately. Since I was out last week, I think returning and leaving again will only serve as a distraction. The last thing I want to do is be a distraction to the kids. Being off last week reminded me of my first priority. I have neglected my duties as a husband and father and I have neglected my health. While I still do not know what my illness is, I do believe stress is major factor. I went to the campus earlier to drop off my laptop, phone, etc., but the office was locked. Fortunately, Mrs. Dee was there, so I left my things with her. I can be reached on my personal cell, if needed.

This experience has been very rewarding. I appreciate having had the opportunity to work for you and our students. The experiences I've had are priceless and I will definitely miss everyone. I wish you and the organization continued success.

Sincerely,

Jacoby White

I felt great about my decision, but I was now facing another harsh reality. I was out of a job. However, I felt a great sense of confidence that I would find a job very soon. The next morning I checked my email and there was no response from Ms. Deeds. She didn't even call. Around noon my phone rang.

"Hello," I answered.

"Hey, man, how are you?" a familiar voice said. It was my good friend Joseph. I had met him during my engineering days at Lucent Technologies.

"What's up man?" I said, happy to hear from him – someone who was not a complaining parent. "I'm good. What have you been up to?"

"Man, I've just been really busy. Are you still working for the charter school?"

"It's funny you ask," I replied with a laugh. "I just resigned yesterday."

"What? You've got to be kidding me." Joseph sounded incredulous. "I'm calling you because I need to hire another engineer. Are you interested in working for me?"

"Am I? Hell yes! What do you need me to do?"

"Come by the office tomorrow and complete your paperwork," he said. "You can start working next week if you want."

"Man, I will be there bright and early tomorrow morning. What kind of hours are we talking about?"

"You set your own hours. You will work from home as well."

"Cool. See you tomorrow."

What a coincidence, I thought. I was unemployed for all of one day. Friday had arrived and I was relaxing on the couch when my phone rang.

"How's it going, Mr. White?" said Mr. Baxter.

"I'm great," I replied. "How about yourself?"

"I have to be honest; I'm a little shocked that you left. I'm really shocked at the way you did it."

"You shouldn't be. You had to have seen it coming."

"I did. But not like this. Ms. Deeds is telling everyone that you took ill. She doesn't want everyone to know that you resigned. She also talked with Mr. Banker. They are trying to figure out how to tell the students and staff. So what are you going to do?"

"I am going to sit back and enjoy life," I said, chuckling.

"What are you going to do as far as a job is concerned?"

"Life is funny like that, Mr. Baxter. I start my new job on Monday."

"Oh, so you had something lined up before you left?"

"Actually, I didn't. It was a blessing."

"Well, congratulations and keep in touch," he said as our conversation ended.

I knew we probably would not talk again. I liked Mr. Baxter, but he was tainted. I knew I couldn't really trust him.

Free at last

Several weeks later I still hadn't heard a peep from Ms. Deeds or Mr. Banker. Weeks turned into months and still no contact. I had settled in my new job and regained freedom. I had gained all my weight back plus some. I felt refreshed. So refreshed that I decided to go to Starbucks for lunch and enjoy an iced caramel macchiato. I was sitting at a table when I heard someone calling my name.

"Mr. White, Mr. White!" said Ms. Winder. "How are you, Mr. White?" She had the biggest smile on her face and I could tell she genuinely missed me.

"I am fine," I said, returning the smile. "How are you?" I pointed to the seat across from mine. "Have a seat, won't you?"

She did and looked up at me. "Where have you been? We miss you. The kids really miss you."

"I've been around."

"I heard you were extremely ill and had to take an indefinite leave of absence."

"I was sick alright," I said. "Sick of that school."

"I understand," she said, nodding. "I know exactly what you mean. A lot of things happened after you left. Mr. Baxter took your place as the Dean of Students. I knew he wanted your position all along. He was just trying to figure out how to get it. I never trusted him."

"How's Ms. Deeds doing?" I asked.

"Oh, she blames you for everything that was wrong with the school. Ms. Deeds told everyone that you turned her school into a reform school for bad kids. She blames you for keeping all the trouble students."

"Now you know that's not true," I said.

"I know, Mr. White. Everyone knew she was lying. She started to panic because she knew she couldn't run the school without you and Mrs. Robinson."

"How's Mrs. Robinson?"

"As far as I know she is still working for the other charter school. But let me finish telling you what happened to Ms. Deeds. Mr. Banker fired her!"

"What?" I erupted.

"Yes, after you left, Mr. Banker hired a guy to monitor Ms. Deeds's every move. He was at the school every day for a month. He reported his findings to Mr. Banker and she was asked to leave. However, the story is that she resigned because of personal reasons."

"Whoa!" I was truly taken aback. "I have to admit that I'm quite shocked."

"That's not even the half of it," she said. "Ms. Deeds has already been replaced."

"By who?"

"Mr. Banker hired a lady from the school district. I believe she was a principal at another school."

"That means he was planning this before I left."

"Probably. Get this, she came through and cleaned house. Half of the staff was let go. Mr. Baxter resigned as well. It seems that when Mr. Baxter took your position, he also received a raise. The new principal questioned his salary since he didn't have a degree and had no teaching experience. She then cut his salary significantly."

"How do you know all this?" I asked.

"Mr. White, I have my sources," she replied with a devilish grin. "He couldn't deal with that, so he started making accusations against Ms. Deeds."

"What kind of accusations?"

"He claimed he wasn't paid for the first month he started working at the school. He is demanding he be paid or else. However, Ms. Deeds is claiming he was volunteering and she gave him a loan during that time period."

"Whoa! It's amazing how they turn on each other when things don't go their way."

"From what I heard, they agreed to pay him, because he has a letter from Ms. Deeds that states his original hiring date." She paused for a minute and looked down at her cup. "You should visit the school, Mr. White. The kids really miss you."

It sounded like a very earnest request, and one that I would seriously consider. "I just may do that, Mrs. Winder."

"Anyway, it was good seeing you, Mr. White," she said, getting up from her seat. "I have to get back to work."

A few months had passed and a new school year had begun. *I think it's time to visit the school,* I thought. As I drove to the school I tried to imagine what kind of response I would get. Would the kids really miss me? *I do feel like I abandoned them.* I could feel the butterflies growing in my stomach as I got closer to the campus. I parked my truck and took a deep breath.

"Okay, here we go," I said to myself. As I entered the building I saw a familiar face. Mrs. Hollins's daughter was the receptionist. She was in college and was working there part-time.

"Hey, Mr. White!" she said as she arose from her chair.

"Hey, young lady! How are you?"

"I'm fine, and yourself?"

"Couldn't be better."

"What are you doing here?" she asked.

"I came to visit," I replied.

"Mr. White…, Mr. White, is that you?" a familiar voice asked. I turned around and saw Mrs. Hollins coming out of her classroom.

"Hey, stranger!" We hugged.

"How are you?" she asked. "Where have you been? You just left us with no warning or explanation."

"I know and I apologize. I'm doing great though."

"Mr. White! Mr. White!" the kids in her classroom screamed as they rushed to me. I was overwhelmed by their response.

"Mr. White!" I heard Mr. Anderson call. "What's up, man?"

"I am doing great," I replied as we embraced.

Mr. Anderson was now the assistant principal and head disciplinarian. "I have your old job. And I don't know if that's a good thing since the last two people in this position are no longer here," he joked. He was referring to Mr. Baxter and me. "Let me show you around…."

As I walked the halls with Mr. Anderson, I could hear the students calling my name from their classrooms. I didn't want to interrupt their classes since most of the teachers didn't know who I was.

"Excuse me," a new teacher said as she approached from behind. "My name is Mrs. Turner and I teach Math."

"Nice to meet you Mrs. Turner," I replied.

"I just wanted to meet you. One of my best students, Tiffany Lewis, just told me that you were the reason she was still at the school."

"Well, I can't take credit for that. She's a hard worker." Actually, I could take credit for that one. Tiffany was a great kid who almost made a huge mistake. She had been bullied by a few girls all year and decided she had had enough. One of the bullies was tormenting her and Tiffany stabbed her in the hand with a pencil. It didn't break the skin fortunately, but she did get her point across. I spent several hours trying to convince the girl's parents that it was an accident.

"Hey Mr. White," said Tiffany as she hid behind the classroom door.

"Hey Tiffany," I said with a big smile on my face.

I have never been good at showing emotion, because my father trained me to be emotionless. However, I was working extremely hard to keep from letting out a tear. As each kid greeted me with hugs, smiles and curious looks I felt overwhelmed with pride and guilt. I was so happy to be back in the presence of the children. However, I felt ashamed for leaving them the way I did. I left the school that day feeling as conflicted as I did when I first quit. However, this time I was happy.

One last thing

My experience working in the school system was life-changing. It gave me a new perspective and appreciation of the opportunities I had been given. I always thought this experience would make a great book or movie. When I made the decision to become a teacher, I believed I knew exactly what our children needed to be successful. Unfortunately, I left with more questions than answers. Each day's unpredictable events would trump those of the previous day. However, I did share some really great moments with the students. I watched many of them flourish in spite of the negativity that surrounded them. Ultimately, I discovered the perpetuator of this negativity was the system itself. I chose to focus this book more on the administration and not the children, because in far too many instances the victim is blamed for his circumstance and not the perpetrator who contributed to or caused it. I do believe that the children need a voice, so their stories can be heard. However, one book would not be nearly enough to explain their plight in full details.

So, what do I believe caused the downfall of this charter school? Well, there are far too many to enumerate, so I will only focus on a few. In my opinion, most charter schools are created because someone believes they can do a better job than the traditional public school systems in educating our children. They argue that the public school system is archaic, noncompetitive and wasteful. Their idea is to create a system that is opposite to the current failing one. One that consists of increased classroom time (more school days and longer hours) and untraditional methods of instruction (no textbook teaching) while being led by younger, more energetic staff. Although this concept sounds attractive, is it really feasible?

Traditional public schools are usually filled with experienced, tenured staff. Experience and wisdom cannot be taught. Please understand, I am not confusing invaluable experience with efficiency. There are some who have been in education for years, but have not positively contributed to the success of their constituents. Why aren't the inefficient senior members of this industry replaced with younger, qualified contributors who are eager to follow and lead? Could it be that the older members of the establishment do not want to move aside or make room for new energy? Are they just content with the status quo? Could this be the reason most proponents of charter schools see a need to create their own schools, thereby establishing their own set of rules and creating new opportunities that don't seem to exist in the traditional public school system.

Will increasing classroom time improve a student's performance? Theoretically, it should. However, something must decrease to accommodate this increase. Teachers and staff must spend more time on the job as well, which will result in a decrease in their quality of life away from the classroom. Most teachers know their job isn't really done when they leave the campus. Most teachers bring their work home. The teachers who have a spouse and/or children at home must sacrifice their personal lives for the good of the school. How long do you think it will take before their job effectiveness suffers? Well, some believe the answer is to hire younger, single teachers and administrators who do not have these commitments. During my short career in teaching, I noticed a turnover rate of 3 to 4 years. It seemed as if the belief was to get as much as you could out of your staff for a short period of time and then replace the ones who flamed out. Could someone really gain enough valuable experience and knowledge in such a small window to make decisions that could steer a person's life? Maybe, there is some value in experience. Did our forefathers understand this when they wrote a minimum age requirement in the constitution for the Presidency? Do we not value the education of our children the way we value our president's experience, even though we tell our kids they too can be president one day?

Let's change our focus to the business of operating a school. The education system has become big business. Or rather, this experience opened my eyes to the realization that it has always been that way. Tax payers have been required to fund a system that has historically failed the majority of its constituents. Why are parents required to fund a system that has not provided much return? Or, is the system producing the result it was intended all along? Is it not in our country's best interest for everyone to be successful? If we were all given the opportunity to maximize our educational experience, who would be willing to settle for minimum wage? How often do you see doctoral candidates working the drive-thru at your local fast food restaurant? I understand that not everyone can be a lawyer, doctor, engineer or scientist. However, who gets to make that decision? In my short time teaching I noticed a premium placed on perfect attendance. Also, being labeled a "Title 1" school was more favorable than being categorized as "Exemplary". I discovered a child could be saddled with numerous "at risk" labels or learning disabilities with the stroke of a pen. However, he or she would have to endure marathon testing to have those same labels removed. Since having a label meant receiving additional funds, why would a school make its removal easy? Just like any business, I understand that a school needs money to survive. Although drastically underpaid, teachers' salaries consume the majority of a school's budget. The remaining dollars, if spent appropriately, are usually exhausted by daily operational costs. However, if money is the driving force, what happens to the well-being of the students? What are the long term effects of unjustly placing a "label" on a child? An administrator once told me that she would retain students just so her numbers looked good for each grade level. Parents were brainwashed into believing their child needed to repeat a grade. This was called "Giving the Gift of Time". Is this a common practice in schools that are successful? Or, is this exploitive technique only used on those who are unaware?

If charter schools are the solution to the ills of the public education system, why aren't more affluent parents lining up to enroll their children? Why are these schools strategically located in low-income, urban areas? Are the schools that focus on assisting minority communities set up to fail? Are the teachers in these schools doomed to fail? I do not believe that teachers are "doomed" to fail. However, they are stepping to the edge of the ravine and are only waiting for a push to plunge to the death of their careers.

Another problem that I have encountered on many occasions is the total lack of accountability on the part of certain staff or teachers. Taking money from the till is a crime in any organization. A thorough and regular verification of the school spending and allocation of funds should be mandatory. If it is not implemented, the parents who pay a portion of their hard earned money to the school for lunches, t-shirts, or any other extras the system could not afford, will be cheated out of their expectation. In essence, the funds allocation should be better regulated and better controlled. Put the need of the children first, not the need of the administration to take money that does not belong to them. School funds should be allocated more efficiently, so that every child benefits from being in school.

In closing, I want clearly state that the corruption and reckless behavior I witnessed during my short time teaching was not exclusive to that campus. There were similar events occurring on several campuses throughout the city. I find it extremely difficult to believe that the overseers of this nationally recognized organization have clean hands.

Date	Vendor	Amount	Description
20081106	JASONS DELI #...	24.68	Instructional Supp...
20081107	AT*BUS PHONE PMT	16.41	Beverages for staff
20081110	PAYPAL *MAC	67.07	Gasoline
20081110	RALSTON DISCOUNT LIQUO	31.39	Beverages for staff
20081110	SHELL OIL 57543442800	40.00	Staff Food-Professional Development
20081110	HEB #063	16.42	Staff Food-Professional Development
20081112	THE FRENCH CORNER	54.48	Office Decor-Holiday supplies; Lights, Christmas
20081112	THE FRENCH CORNER 00013367		
	20090216 COCHON RESTAURANT	$39.64	Food while in New Orleans for school leader retreat
20090214	WAFFLE HOUSE 1010100000	$17.15	Food While traveling during School leader retreat,
20090213	DISCOUNT ZONE 1206	$54.44	Gasoline for traveling while in New Orleans for school
20090216	MOTHER'S RESTAURANT	$94.08	Food while in new orleans, for school leader retreat
20090216	K PAULS LOUISIANA KITC	$42.73	Food while in new orleans
20090216	W NEW ORLEANS	$43.26	lodging cost while at school leader retreat
20090217	RITA MAE'S KITCHEN	$58.03	food while in new orleans for school leader retreat
20090216	EXXONMOBIL 423560652	$46.34	Gasoline for traveling while in New Orleans for School
20090217	HERTZ RENTAL-CAR	$151.57	Car rental for travel to New Orleans to school leader re
20090217	W NEW ORLEANS	$92.71	Valet parking at hotel while at school leader retreat in
20081209	EDIBLE ARRANGEMENTS	64.00	Thank you gift for meeting with school leader about ne
20081211	EDIBLE ARRANGEMENTS #7	49.50	Thank you gift for meeting with school leader about ne
20090525	EDIBLE ARRANGEMENTS #7	26.88	Death in the family for serving the school in capacities of b
20090227	EXXONMOBIL	106.36	Gift of appreciation
20081030	EXXONMOBIL 47186499	78.59	Gift of Appreciation
20090406	EXXONMOBIL 47498340	232.00	Student appreciation
	EXXONMOBIL 96549555	162.00	Gasoline f...

• In 1998, voters in HISD approved $678 million.

• In 2002, voters in HISD approved $808.6 million.

• In 2002, voters in HISD approved $805 million.

• In 2012, HISD seeks $1.89 billion.

• Grand total of $4.18 billion in less than 15 yrs.

Item E-1 - Approval For The Consolidation Of James D. Ryan Middle School A ⌄

Houston & Texas > News > Houston

HISD will close Ryan, tables plan to merge two high schools

By Ericka Mellon March 7, 2013 Updated: March 8, 2013 1 00am

"Do you think you would have passed that bond had you told them you were going to close schools?" Sterling graduate Dikombi Gite asked the board

Bond Not Used for Its Original Intent

Grimes and Rhoades Elementary, both high performing schools, received a combined total of over $7M from the 2007 bond. However, in 2011, HISD decided to close them and reallocate over $6M of unused bond money to several schools without the communities approval. $1.2M was given towards a dormant communications program at Yates High School. $50k was given to Shearn Elementary

www.youtube.com/watch?v=Z_px3oQf2Cc

www.youtube.com/watch?v=VR2x5t00g7U

201

www.ingramcontent.com/pod-product-compliance
Lightning Source LLC
LaVergne TN
LVHW051516080426
835509LV00017B/2080